Talking to the Earth

By Gordon MacLellan

Talking to the Earth

©1995 Gordon MacLellan

ISBN 1 898307 43 1

Cover design by Daryth Bastin
Cover illustration by Gordon MacLellan

Published by:

Capall Bann Publishing
Freshfields
Chieveley
Berks
RG20 8TF

Tel/Fax 01635 248711

Dedication:

to the Earth that is my joy and inspiration and the fire in my spirit

Acknowledgement:

This book goes out with many thanks to all the people who have put up with me over the years and offered support and opportunity especially the Mersey Valley Countryside Warden Service and Cate and Malcolm.

These colleagues and all the children, old and young, who have played in the wild and the countryside and have given "Talking to the Earth" the chance to be.

The extract from "Willow" on p46 is by kind permission of H Llewellyn-Williams and Poetry Wales Press

Haiku on p78 from are reprinted with permission of Penguin Books

Celtic verses on p79, 80 are reprinted with permission of Routledge

"The Song of Amergin" p82 is reprinted with permission of Colin Smythe Ltd

Talking to the Earth: Worksheets

A set of 20 A4 size worksheets are available to accompany this book.

Printed on heavy, white paper, these are designed as photocopy originals for use in the classroom or with your group in other situations.

Each worksheet includes Leader's Notes for the activity on one side and illustrations for that activity on the other.

To obtain a worksheet set, send an order with a cheque for £7.00 (post free in the U.K.), made payable to Capall Bann Publishing, to:

Capall Bann Publishing
Freshfields
Chieveley
Berks
RG20 8TF

CONTENTS

Apache USA ← masks → Papua New Guinea
from →
Dogon, Australia
Africa

FOREWORD

Welcome to "Talking to the Earth".
This is a book of celebration. Despite all that is amiss in our human world and in our relationship with the rest of the world we live among, life is still a wonderful thing and something to take delight in. For me, one of the first, and most important roles for environmental education is to remind people of the joy that is in life and to help people explore and express that. Hopefully, this book will be one tool for people trying to do just that.

"Talking..." is incomplete - even while writing it, I know that there are materials on costumes and face painting that have not got in and the complex, river-flowing patterns of celebration planning waiting to run across a page. Maybe next time? And nothing here is fixed - take "Talking"s activities as ideas to think about and play with, but not as rules to be obeyed. The book is also inhabited by Boggarts for no good reason other than that they wanted to be here.

Activities about making and doing, jumping up and down and singing songs with colour and shape: take these as ways of talking to the earth: giving shape to feelings about ourselves and this planet home.

Walk in peace, dance in beauty, enjoy it all.

Boggarts in Head Sculptures

the workbox
boggart... the
reason why
nothing is
ever quite
where you
left it...

TALKING TO THE EARTH

We live in a world surrounded by excitement and delight. There is
beauty to be found and a sense of wonder to experience everywhere we
go. From the strange silhouettes of an industrial estate, to the challenge
of a weed in a pavement, from the most elegant forest to the wildest
storm, we are part of a world that offers so much to explore, so much to
inspire.

Often it seems that somewhere along the road of "growing up" we lose
touch with that appreciation and we let our experience become chan-
nelled along more mundane avenues. One of the fundamental challenges
facing environmental education is to help people step out of that path to
separation from their world, and renew, and keep renewing their meeting
with the world they live in. We need to peel away - or prevent arriving
in the first place, some of those layers of conditioning that wrap up our
hearts and minds and enjoy the world afresh.

Scientific investigation can lead to the understanding of processes,
awareness exercises can sharpen sensitivity and art can help us explore
the abstract. The path to the heart of the person, where the most lasting
and strongest decisions are made, needs all of those aspects to combine
into an integrated journey of experience. And with that, we need to
recognise the spiritual: the deep personal experience of nature that arises
from effective environmental education and requires its own time and
space to be appreciated. Environmental education is about change:
encouraging people to understand their world and where they belong in
it, to appreciate the wonder and diversity of it and to be prepared to
make their own informed decisions about what they feel should happen
to it. All that changes the person and we need to be ready to address
those changes as much as we set up the learning situations that bring
them about.

This book is a mixed collection of "art" and "spirit" activities. Some are wholly art-based and are designed as ways of expressing understanding or feelings about the natural world, while in others, the creative work is the endpiece of a process of personal discovery.

THE TESTING GROUND
These activities have grown, been tried, changed and tried again over a number of years - predominantly with groups of children in south Manchester but also with various groups all over the UK. Activities were designed mostly for use with groups of about 30 children with a couple

---

Activity Checklist

Key concept:

environmental awareness : an activity should draw upon environmental experience and offer a personal way of interpreting that without judgements of "right" and "wrong"

Activities were also expected to be/show:

non-discriminatory: make no assumption about, race, sex, mobility, etc. of children.

non-violent: should not promote aggressive or destructive behaviour

simple technology: having done an activity once with a leader, a child should be able to go away and with a minimum of help, do it again for themselves.

not leader intensive: techniques and concepts should be able to be explained easily to a class as a whole

low environmental impact: not leave lasting damage or disruption to a site

use recycled/natural materials: wherever possible, consumption of materials is minimised and careful use of natural resources is promoted.

8

of adults and were aimed at 8 - 12 year olds. Situations ranged from formal school workshops - either in school or in the field to small public events and large free-wheeling playschemes involving several hundred children. With some modification, most at one time or another have been used with older or younger groups.

SOURCES OF MATERIAL
Most of these activities grew as hybrid shoots from seeds drawing together ideas and experiences from many sources and many people.

A number are rooted in concepts drawn from indigenous peoples from around the world. In these cultures, the bonds between people and place are often much more immediate and deeply rooted in the individual than we are used to. People there are much more aware of their relationship to and dependance upon the natural world for their daily survival. The lessons we can learn from these ideas of "connectedness" are invaluable: they can link us as individuals, personally and intimately with the world we live in; reinforcing the awareness that nothing we can do can ever actually divorce us from the world we live upon.

The experiences such activities offer people are not intended to dictate a particular worldview - they are about individual personal awareness of the world that person walks in. Later those experiences may remain tucked away inside that person's heart and spirit or may be interpreted in the light of personal or cultural beliefs, but in this situation, they are there for the individual's own inspiration. To appreciate another perspective is not necessarily to adopt it, and we can work with tribal ideas without betraying the roots these are drawn from or feeling we are compromising our own beliefs. It is, however, equally important to present other alternatives as viable concepts about the world we live in in their own rights. It can be all too easy to adopt a rather superior "western, scientific, materialist" attitude to a worldview that speaks of spirit in earth, animal and tree and that knows that each of us is totem linked to different aspects of that world that surrounds us. Watch how you yourself think of these attitudes as that is what a group will pick up. Just as, when you are telling a story, you need to be able to see/feel/live inside the story as you tell it, so if you are describing the power of a songline, do so with the Songline alive and vibrant and real for you - if only for that space of time.

That is all much easier said than done: essentially if you approach these activities and ideas with the view that they are all a lot of nonsense, go away and think again. But if you are intrigued, excited or just plain interested your own sense of eager curiosity can bring a group to watching a puppet take shape in a wood and walk and talk with laughter and delight at the magic of it, and the silliness, without mocking the apparent simple-mindedness of it.

And if challenged, you could always ask which of the many worldviews that surround us have actually had least destructive impact upon the environments they have evolved in?

USING THESE ACTIVITIES

Most of these activities were designed to fit into 1 - 2 hour slots in longer workshop sessions or events. In such situations, groups were usually involved in developing scenarios where a storyline was explored through a series of activities during a day, often leading to some sort of performance at the end. You can, of course, adapt things in whatever way feels appropriate to your situation but the processes described below may offer ideas to build into your own planning.

In a classroom and other contexts this format may not always be appropriate - we were producing "complete package" sessions, meeting a group for just that day and offering an experience from start to finish. In situations with more relaxed timetables, the headlong charge that swept a story through a day sprouting wild performances like mushrooms en route may not be needed and ideas can be explored in a more leisurely fashion.

The exploring/investigating side of many of these activities calls for the opportunity for children to have the chance to roam and crawl, get grubby and have adventures. In planning this sort of work, you, as leader, need to know the site, know the tricky bits, plants to warn people of - for safety's sake and the plants' sake, and so on. You are also responsible for adult support and supervision: don't let the goups in your care wander where they will out of your site: either work within an area where people are always in sight or have enough helpers to be able to split up and explore in small groups, each with an adult in tow...But whatever you do, don't **not** go out because you are worried about the organisation of an expedition. Helpers can be found, headteachers, troupe leaders or whatever convinced and there is a whole world waiting for an adventure.

When planning sessions, we aimed to work with a "storyline" that would capture the imagination and give excitement and child-centred direction to a connected series of activities.   The underlying patterns used in planning workshops are quite straightforward and could be applied to all sorts of situations: most educators probably use them already.

Stages used in structuring a workshop
1. Set the scene: usually a story would be used - accepting the role of magic, the "suspension of disbelief" to recruit the group to a cause, give them a purpose. This does not need to be serious, or even very directive (see the examples later) - nor does it have to use a story....invitations to attend a "Garden's Party" might arrive, calling for the participation of a pond on sticks or a singing flowerbed; "secret instructions" might be issued and "your mission, should you choose to accept it, is to determine what was happening in this place 100 (or 50 or 150) years ago, and present this in silence to the rest of your company".
2. Investigate: the sense of purpose that the above brings is used to determine the shape of investigative work: it would usually be up to the group, sometimes with a lot of help, to decide for themselves what the parameters of their study should be - what do they need to know about pond animals, how could they count the number of flowers in a field, in what form should they record their information?

3. Create: discussion of information gathered above is used to inform an expressive activity - creativity now draws upon direct observation and deduction and can then feed a degree of inspiration personal reflection back to the results of the investigation.

4. Perform: having embarked upon a "mission", it becomes important to complete the circle - the "Garden's Party" needs to happen - those flowerbeds will sing!

There was often, particularly in Performance sections, and with larger groups of people, another layer of planning structures designed to create choreographic skeletons upon which the creative work of large numbers of people producing unpredictable results could be placed to give exciting and coherent finished pieces. This work will be developed in other publications and is not so absolutely necessary for smaller groups.

Planning summary

section	aim	hints
setting	give purpose	be imaginative, not dictative
investigation	determine what we need to know	guide gently
	find it	advise on techniques
creating	use this to shape something that matches the "purpose"	handle with care
performance	complete the mission	go for it!

TOTEMS

In many societies, while we individuals live and walk as humans, we are also, personally, linked to members of other species: spiritual brothers and sisters to completely different animals. That other species is one's totem - it may be a "real" animal or plant or rock, or it may exist only in the non-physical world of spirits and enchantment.

A native Australian child, for example, named into a Wallaby clan is linked to other Wallaby humans in her own tribe and to others across tribal boundaries, and to animal wallabies. For their animal kin, Wallaby people will perform certain ceremonies to support the animals in their passage through life and Wallaby humans will probably never be involved in the hunting or eating of animal wallabies.

In western culture, totemism has largely vanished but you could explore its traces in the animals seen on coats of arms, in family or place names and stories. Totems may be linked to individuals, or families, or whole tribal groups - animals associated with Highland clans and on coats of arms may well be left-over totems.

The full weight of totemism is probably inappropriate for use in our situations, but that idea that everyone can find their own personal bond with nature is a very powerful one. Trying, if only for a short while, to appreciate life and its problems from another species' perspective is a telling exercise and a good way of bringing people to a realisation of what the rest of the world needs from us - rather than what we may want to take from the rest of the world!

ENVIRONMENTAL AWARENESS

Many of the activities here depend upon direct environmental experience for their inspiration and their impact upon participants. We need to get right down there and enjoy crawling around under a hedge to really produce the puppets of the characters who might just be lurking there, out of sight behind the twisted hawthorn trunks.

In recent years, activities leading people into new discoveries of local, apparently familiar, places have grown new branches and flowered into some wonderful and exciting forms. Discussion and descriptions of this work are to be found in particular in the books of Steve van Matre and the Institute for Earth Education and Joseph Bharat Cornell. For our purposes, we need to draw upon "discovery" activities: those that involve giving the senses reminders of how amazing the world around us is - especially where we can rediscover places that we thought we knew, finding whole new realms of interest in the school wildlife garden, or the park down the road. The Institute's work goes beyond this into dealing with ecological concepts in innovative ways but for our work here in exploring the natural world through personal creativity, those initial "discovery" types of activity are fine as starting points.

OUR ROLE AS TEACHERS AND LEADERS

Throughout the activities in this book, the challenge to us as group leaders, is to facilitate the growth of ideas and inspiration. Often the most helpful thing to do, once an activity is running is to simply keep people talking and thinking: unless it is a simple technical point, avoid telling people what they should do - encourage them to decide what is best for what they want to do. What is the picture in their head that they are trying to express - don't catch yourself imposing your ideas upon theirs.

Some activities: **Tokens, Mapsticks,** and **Story-shields** for example, all work as memory triggers to help their makers tell the stories of their experiences. In doing so, we tap into long traditions of oral culture:

going through the process of making and telling is a strong confidence and communication exercise for children. To then tell them to "write it all down" can rob the activity of that strength and bring it crashing back to yet another piece of school-work. Be careful how you handle follow-up work, take an idea onward rather than just regurgitate it in a different form.

INTEGRATING WITH OTHER WORK

Environmental education can be a strangely misty subject: it is there, the experiences it offers hit you and your group like elephants but other than some of the more obvious subject areas, it can be very hard to pin down what a group gets out of the sort of multi-disciplinary projects described here.

When planning workshops of this sort, we used, and still use, a system taken from the Manchester City Council Education Authority "Cross Curricular Themes, Skills, Dimensions" publications to explore the range and classroom relevance of different workshops. These bring together two planning formats: a "matrix" that helps us lay out the bare bones of a single activity or a whole workshop and the "turtle" that can be used to relate matrix activities to curriculum areas, although it was designed for planning longer term school topics. Two worked examples are given below: one for a "Mapsticks and Songlines" day and the other for a pollution workshop called "The White Trout". Other workshop scenarios are given with some chapters setting out aims, story-lines and activities (see **The Boggarts' Gifts** and **Beavers, Crows and Mosqui-toes**, for example) but the full matrix/turtle layouts are only given for these two.

THE WHITE TROUT

Aim: to look at measuring and assessing the impact of water pollution involving stories and creative work.

Group: various classes of 10 -12 year olds from inner city and southern Manchester on day visits to a local country park.

ACTIVITY BREAKDOWN:
title, activities, content. (After "Implementing the Whole Curriculum", MCC Ed. Dept)

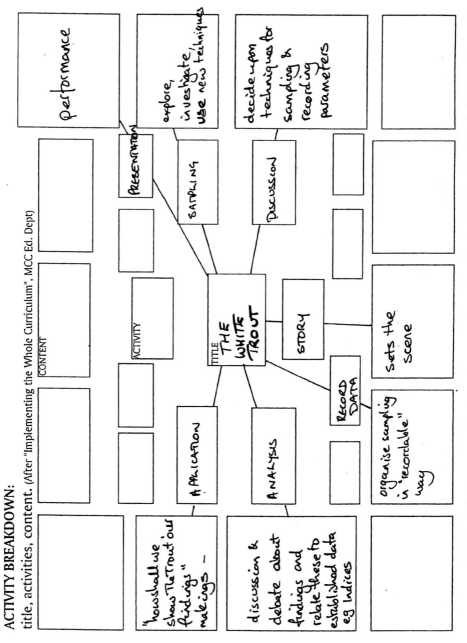

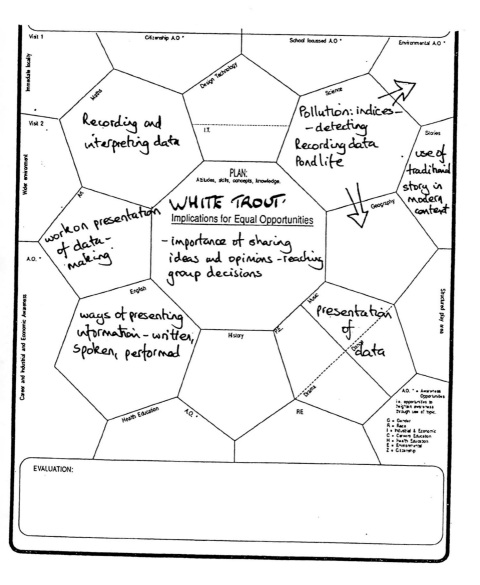

Visit 1   Citizenship A.O *   School focussed A.O *   Environmental A.O *

Immediate locality

Visit 2

Wider environment

Maths

Design Technology

Recording and interpreting data

I.T.

Science

Pollution: indices – – detecting Recording data Pond life

Stories

use of traditional story in modern context

PLAN:
Attitudes, skills, concepts, knowledge.

Art

work on presentation of data – making

A.O.

WHITE TROUT·
Implications for Equal Opportunities

– importance of sharing ideas and opinions – reaching group decisions

Geography

English

PE

Music

Presentation of data

Career and Industrial and Economic Awareness

ways of presenting information – written, spoken, performed

History

Drama

Design

Structured play area

Health Education

A.O. *

RE

A.O. * = Awareness
Opportunities
i.e. opportunities to
heighten awareness
through use of topic.

G = Gender
R = Race
I = Industrial & Economic
C = Careers Education
H = Health Education
E = Environmental
Z = Citizenship

EVALUATION:

17

Setting the scene: the day begins with an old Irish story wherein a forlorn princess turns herself into a magical white trout to spend eternity hunting through the rivers and lakes of Ireland for her drowned lover. Now, however, her search has spread to the Mersey where she is hovering around in the Irish Sea, unsure of where she could swim in our area, but having heard rumours that her prince has been seen here, Would the group help work out just where a trout, a fish of clean waters, could go a-searchin'?

Getting going: much discussion usually followed this while the class worked out its criteria for assessing water quality. Children were encouraged to explore any avenue that they felt would give some indication: general appearance, litter, aquatic and marginal plants, large animals, underwater life...

The investigation: once an initial set of parameters were established, the class would usually split up and different groups sample different water bodies within a given area. A range of basic equipment was available (pond nets, trays, bottles, clipboards, handlenses, etc) and groups were encouraged to devise ways of recording data so that different groups could effectively compare results.

Analysis: when the class reassembled, extra information was made available - ideas about "pollution indicator species" and diversity indices were introduced (most groups had already made some qualitative decisions about clean/dirty water animals). With further discussion, the class decided upon the relative cleanliness of the waters sampled and recommended a choice of areas for the Trout to visit.

Application: it was then pointed out that no trout, however magical, was really likely to be able to read and the class were asked to turn their results into visual form which would be quite clear to any passing fish. Again, a mixture of materials was available and some techniques suggested (**Fat Fish on Sticks** and **Crazy Hats...** both proved popular).

Presentation: the day would then end with a grand performance of "polluted and not-so-polluted places" combining visual arts work with some movement ideas. performances ranged from simple processions of people representing different ponds to cameo presentations of "what would happen if you visited this pond".

Overall: some initial disbelief at the improbability of the story usually disappeared fairly quickly and groups either went with the fantasy element of it all or simply played along with the sheer silliness of it all when seen from another stance. the repeated challenge of gathering and analysing information and then "translating" it for a totally different intelligence drew people on and added a further challenge beyond the usual pond-dip/pollution analysis work. Allowing the group to determine their own investigation parameters gave them a much stronger commitment to the work - they were keen to see what their ideas could show.

MAPSTICKS AND SONGLINES
Aim: to incorporate work on local geography with ideas from other cultures about local places and landscapes. Later, the whole activity came to be used more as a language and communications exercise.

Group: "Mapsticks" has run with slightly different formats with classes ranging from 6 year olds right through to "A"Level Geography students. On the whole, it has been used with 8 - 12 year olds.

Setting the scene: talk about journeys, read from Norton Juster's *The Phantom Tollbooth* on "the best reason for going from one place to another is to see what's in-between", discuss journeys that everyone has taken - perhaps describe daily journeys to school.

Exploration: getting to know the site: small groups of people scatter across a site, each picking out their own trail towards a final meeting point: this might involve following a map, going on a discovery walk or simply having a ramble. People are encouraged to watch and talk on the way: what do I see? what is most noticeable? how could I tell someone else where I have been?

On their journey, people collect landmark tokens - rushes from round a pond perhaps, a leaf from a significant tree.

Analysis: at a prearranged meeting point the class reassembles and people settle down to sort out their finds and start telling their journey to someone else (or to themselves) - this helps organise both the sequence and important features in their heads. A mapstick is introduced (if it did not appear earlier while setting the scene).

Application: individuals now work to create their own mapstick record of their travels.

Presentation 1: people join up with folk from other groups to share stories, describing their journey as recorded on their mapstick. The whole class will listen to several journeys and might finish with a walking song to set them on their way home again.

Presentation 2: on longer sessions the group would move into turning their group journeys into songlines so that by the end of a day, they can sing their way across the site and with a number of songs from different groups, we can have the whole place mapped by music. Further discussion then starts working out what we should do where songlines cross....

Overall: a very versatile workshop that can be changed readily to suit the needs of the group. The strength of a mapstick as a personal token should not be overlooked - they become treasured and their stories recounted for many months.

ACTIVITY BREAKDOWN:

title, activities, content. (After "Implementing the Whole Curriculum", MCC Ed. Dept)

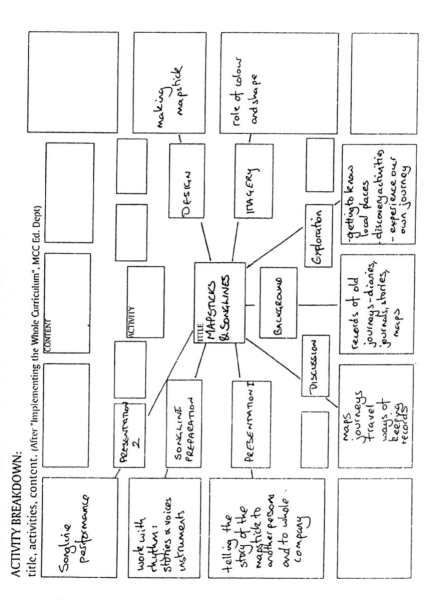

CONTENT

ACTIVITY

making mapstick

role of colour and shape

DESIGN

IMAGERY

Exploration
- getting to know local places
- discovery activities
- experience our own journey

TITLE:
MAPSTICKS & SONGLINES

BACKGROUND

records of old journeys - diaries, journals, stories, maps

DISCUSSION

maps
journeys
travel
ways of keeping records

PRESENTATION 2

SONGLINE PREPARATION

PRESENTATION I

Songline Performance

work with rhythm: stories & voices instruments

telling the story of the mapstick to another person and to whole company

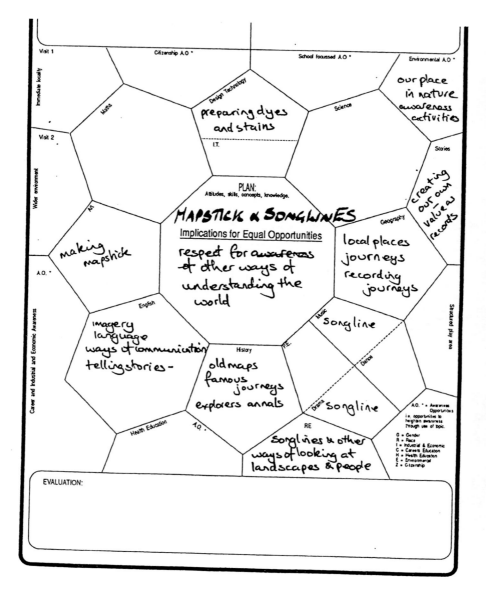

Visit 1

Immediate locality

Citizenship A.O.*

School focussed A.O.*

Environmental A.O.*

Design Technology

preparing dyes and stains

Maths

Science

our place in nature awareness activities

Visit 2

I.T.

Stories

Wider environment

PLAN:
Attitudes, skills, concepts, knowledge.

creating our own value a records

Art

MAPSTICK & SONGLINES

Implications for Equal Opportunities

Geography

local places journeys recording journeys

making mapstick

respect for awareness of other ways of understanding the world

A.O.*

English

Music

Songline

Career and Industrial and Economic Awareness

imagery language ways of communication telling stories -

History

old maps famous journeys explorers annals

P.E.

Dance

Songline

Structured play area

Drama

Songline

Health Education

A.O.

RE

A.O.* = Awareness Opportunities
i.e. opportunities to heighten awareness through use of topic.

G = Gender
R = Race
I = Industrial & Economic
C = Careers Education
H = Health Education
E = Environmental
Z = Citizenship

songlines & other ways of looking at landscapes & people

EVALUATION:

22

GETTING READY

Activities and worksheets

The various activities in this book are grouped more or less by subject into chapters usually with some background and general principles relating to that topic. To work with an activity you do not necessarily need to take on board the wider or deeper implications that may go with it, but bearing these in mind and using the session as a springboard to more discussion or personal reflection adds much more weight to the impact of an activity.

Where appropriate, chapters contain both "Leaders' Notes" with advice on materials, length of activity, suggested ways of organising your group and so on, and notes on the activities themselves. The individual chapter format does tend to change a bit to suit the activities therein. The activity notes are presented as working guides, but as with most group sessions, do not just leave people to get on with any activity - make sure you have tried it first! A number of the activities have also been drafted as A4 sized worksheet photocopy originals and are available as a pack: "Talking to the Earth Worksheets". In any one chapter, activities described elsewhere in this book are named in **bold** type.

In preparing for using these activities some outlines of the commoner materials and basic equipment requirements might be helpful. Throughout the Leaders' Notes a "basic kit" is referred to: a standard set of essential bits and pieces, invaluable to the leader leaping out into the grass, paint and glue of environmental creativity. Here follows the contents of this leader's magical box and ideas of some other valuable additions to the art cupboard.

The Basic Kit - for a group of 30 or so children.
> **1 tool box** - to hold as much as possible
> **heavy duty "gaffer" tape** - 1 roll

children's scissors - 20+ pairs (including several left-handed or equal weighted ones)

larger scissors - 2 pairs

PVA glue - a couple of jars

assorted **tubs of paint**,(mix with glue and a bit of water to go further and be waterproof on drying, and generally to conserve supplies)

a ball of **string**

several reels of **twine**

a **stapler** or two - with staples that fit!

masking tape - several rolls

paper fasteners - a box of several hundred

a bundle of 30 **peasticks**

assorted useful **exciting bits** - beads, feathers, strange little twiddly things

some **magic markers** - big fat colourful ones

pencils - 30

file cards - 60 (or scrap card of that general size)

paintbrushes - 20 or more

heavy craft knife - 2, attached to the leader (and another adult helper) by a long piece of string

a First Aid Kit

a tarpaulin - rolled up and carried by some willing volunteer

the workbox boggart... the reason why nothing is ever quite where you left it...

Materials Generally

If you are stocking up on supplies from scratch, perhaps notes from playscheme shopping lists would help.

GLUES

PVA - 5 litre cartons - strong and essential - dilute for most uses. Give it time to dry - it washes out when wet but is waterproof when dry.
Copydex - more specialised and more expensive - good for rubbery skins when scraped over cloth and for working with foam

TAPE

Gaffer - "waterproof cloth tape" - expensive, but invaluable, so be mean with it and make its use count. Get from Scrapstores (see below), or maybe industrial suppliers. Shop around for the cheapest supply
Masking - the basic tape for most work here, again try your Scrapstore. Go for 12, 19 or 25 mm widths for most work and buy in bulk
Double-sided sticky - expensive but useful on occasion

FASTENERS

Staplers - standard school ones should do. Make sure you've got lots of staples
Staple-gun - useful sometimes but perilous. Guard it fiercely
Paper-fasteners/split-pins - 12, 25 and 35mm lengths are all useful. Remember to work fasteners away from skin - ends should always open on the outside of a mask or whatever; although you can cover the ends with masking tape.
String - parcel string, baler twine, rope - whatever size it is, someone will use it eventually - but baler and parcel are good to have in quantity
Thread - "carpet thread" and "button twine" both come on 100 or 50m reels if you hunt around - useful strong threads for more delicate constructions

STICKS

Peasticks - those thin fawn or green 30 - 45cm stakes sold to support plants. Buy by the hundred - try Scrapstores rather than Garden Centres

Bamboo canes - a range of sizes is always useful. If 3m+ ones are available buy them and always retrieve them at the end of an event.

Withies - very slender, 1 - 2m stripped willow canes. Usually available from Scrapstores, they need to be damped down before use, after which they can be gently bent into all manner of shapes. Obtain in bulk from specialist suppliers - sold by the bundle - ask for "6 foot, buff willow", Fresh, green willow has not had its bark stripped and needs to be used very quickly. Local countryside rangers or other land managers may be able to help out with a range of sizes of fresh withies if they are growing willow coppice (and if they are not, encourage them to do so!)

OTHER THINGS TO GET LOTS OF

Drawing materials - wax crayons, coloured and graphite pencils, felt-tip pens, charcoal...and don't forget the pencil sharpeners!

Paints - ready mixed bottles are easiest, metallic powder paints are great for effects on damp surfaces (use them dry) and if you are feeling rich go for lustre (slightly iridescent) and vitreous (work on glass and plastic) paints for that special touch

Paper - coloured sugar, newsprint, crepe, anything that is going, really.

Tissue - coloured and plain - large sheets of white tissue are available quite cheaply by the ream from packaging suppliers. More specialised, but tougher tissues are more expensive

Cardboard - avoid buying as you can usually scrounge quantities of the stuff! Go for a range of sizes, not too battered and not so thick that you can't cut it with a craft knife

DOMESTIC BITS

Wash it, sniff it, wash it again and get as many as you can: yogurt pots, margarine tubs, large plastic bottles, old sheets, egg boxes, wrapping paper, old umbrellas (no, don't wash the last three) - use your imagination

OTHER EXCITING AND USEFUL BITS
A list here could go on indefinitely. You need to cultivate the habits of a hoarder, on as big a scale as you can manage as all sorts of things just accumulate and those huge sheets of plastic, the lumps of foam rubber, assorted hub-caps, several hundred plastic ducks from the Scrapstore are all bound to come in useful one day.......

SCRAPSTORES
Many local Play Associations, as well as providing sources of advice, training in new ideas and contacts with people doing interesting things, can supply cheap materials to their members. Make contact with (and join) your local Association - perhaps through the local Council's Leisure, Recreation or Social Services Department. Then, as well as spending all your pennies in supporting a good cause, you can encounter the delights of "scrap" - remarkable, unexpected, stimulating and safe materials often donated by local industry. It is generally not wise to visit a Scrapstore except when accompanied by someone of great restraint and when driving a very small vehicle, or on public transport where trailing yards of excess whatever will not be permitted...

GETTING GOING

Whether you have just walked in to face the group you have been seeing daily for what feels like an eternity, or this is your first encounter with these people, and perhaps even their first meeting with each other, some sort of group "warm-up, say hello, let go and go for it" activity is often called for. Not always, but often. It starts the ideas rolling, sets a mood and, hopefully, relaxes and brings people to talk to and work with each other.

There are countless "ice-breaker" and "warm-up" activities in many other publications and to repeat many of them here would become tedious. The success of a "warm-up" depends very much upon how comfortable you, as a leader, are with that activity and how relevant it is to the situation the group is in. Look around and find the ones that you enjoy working with - try some of those given below and hunt more widely as well.

CHOOSING WARM-UPS
Activities you use to make contact and get a group going could or should:
~ be simple and quick to "teach"
~ have minimal equipment needs
~ be enjoyable - for you and the group
~ be gently challenging (don't shock people yet)
~ affirm the individual - do not isolate or estrange
~ be relevant in some degree to the day's theme
~ give your group a sense of confidence in you as the person they will listen to for the rest of the session

Leaders' Notes
Time & Materials: most of the following activities require no materials and last 5 - 10 minutes. Depending upon how far you go with them, they could last longer
Organisation: these are all designed to be used with a whole group of

about 30 people - although they will often call for people to separate into pairs or small groups. The pattern should always come back to whole company: a pulse of everyone - pairs - small groups - then everyone again.

Most of the instructions here are given as if they are being delivered to a group

NAMES
1. Introductions I
Sitting in a circle, tell your name and something about yourself to the person sitting next to you (what you had for breakfast, a secret ambition, where you have come from, greatest achievement...). Then introduce that person to the circle at large.

2. Introductions II
Follow I above with the leader crossing the circle to introduce someone else, maybe just with their name (if you can't remember it, ask it again!) to the company. That person can then cross to another individual and introduce them, who then finds someone else.....A sort of cascade is set up which ends up with everyone having changed places and having tried to remember another new name.

3. Introductions III
Cross the circle and clap hands with someone while you each say the other's name. Change places and the second person goes to name another. Build up the greeting:
> clap hands
> clap hands over heads
> clap while both jump
> add a hop, skip or jump as you cross the circle
> speed the whole thing up

4. Animal Introductions

Cross the circle as a particular animal and greet another person as your animal might (add noises). Change places while the second person takes your animal and changes it to one of their own as they go off to meet someone, or something, else. If you can build names into your grunts, squeaks and hisses all to the good and the sense of silliness.

5. Passing Games

And bring in all those familiar games tossing a ball, or whatever, to each other around a circle, calling the name of your chosen target. Introduce several balls so people need to be extra alert. Alternatively, for a more intimate session, pass a sponge ball round the circle from one person to another without the use of hands and without the ball touching the ground. Try passing from foot to foot, chin to elbow, without using limbs....

NAMES AND RHYTHMS
6. Clapping Names

Establish names with positive, or at least cheerful, descriptions - Athletic Anna, Hilarious Harry...Gallumphing Gordon. Go round your circle and have each person introduce themselves - with the whole company calling their name back to them. In a second round, each person could step forward and add a movement or gesture to their name, which, with the name, is again repeated by the whole company.

Now give people a minute or two to sort out the rhythm of their name and to try clapping it.
For example:

	Ath - - let - - ic	Ann -- a
	slow quick quick	slow slow
or	Hil - - ar - - i - - ous	Harr -- y
	4 x quicks...............	slow slow

Try experimenting with the different sounds your hands make by clapping against different bits of the hand - palm, heel, cupped.

When people are happy with their clapping names:
Round 3: each person says and claps their name and the company repeats this to them
Round 4: just the clapping this time, no voices.

7. A Name Symphony
Now become a conductor. Each person will clap only their own name rhythm and once started will go on repeating this until you signal them to stop. Start at one point in the circle, and gradually bring the rest of the company in one by one, letting each new name be clapped several times over before cuing in the following person. Eventually, the whole company will all be clapping their own names.
Take it in turns to pop into the middle of the circle at this point and listen to the sound of the whole company. The final effect can be surprising in its sense of cohesion.

8. Manic Molehills
The above two activities could be repeated with names and adjectives appropriate to the rest of a workshop session with the final name symphony becoming a rhythm to create a performance around later. For example, "elongated earthworm", "munching millipede" and "fuzzy fungus" all came out of "Manic Molehills" - an activity about earth.

9. Working Together
Set up a steady beat: 1, 2, 3, 4 marked with hand-claps or gently stamping feet.
Go round the circle and invite each person to improvise a set of claps within that 4-space with the rest of the company repeating the rhythm afterwards before the lead moves on.

The **name symphony** format can be used to build this up to another performance.

VOICES

Overall: work on opening up lungs and throats, relaxing chest and throat muscles, breathing deeply. Start with a good yawn and a stretch.

10. Soundscapes

Sit in silence, maybe in half-light and dream a little. Listen to sounds around the group, or talk the group gently into a feeling of where they will be working - what would it be like to rest, as a fish, among the plants at the bottom of a pond, perhaps. Let everyone bring back a sound from this place, some small sound like captures some part of their feeling of the place.

On a count of 4, everyone makes their sound, softly. Then they do their own 4-count (to themselves, not out loud) and repeat their sound. As everyone counts at different rates, the sounds gradually separate. Listen to the picture, the atmosphere, the company begins to create with their soundscape.

11. Vowels

Go operatic, and call extra long vowel sounds to each other across the circle - go for projection and clarity of sound. Work through A E I O and U together first and then let everyone throw individual vowels at each other. Have conversations using only vowels.

Try walking around while vowelling at each other. Call greetings to each other, team up with people making similar sounds to have a brief im-promptu choir. Enjoy it.

11. Words

See how much expression you can wring from a single word in much the same way as vowels. Almost any word will do: "rhubarb", "rice-pud-ding" and "tree" have all worked well.

Slow words down, send them high, bury them low, repeat them short and sharp...

SHAPES AND PICTURES

"warming up" people's imaginations can take many forms. if you are planning sessions more on drawing and making than performance, you might like to bring in a couple of the following - but even if people are going to be working in these media a physically lively start to a session is a good way of relaxing everyone. Remember there is no "right" or "wrong" here - your job is to encourage people to express themselves - not to act as some fine art critic.

If we take a theme of "trees" and see what we might do...

12. Big Bits Of Paper

Use fat wax crayons or broad magic markers and let each person fill a large piece of paper with shape and colour - go for the feel of the thing not accurate representation. For shape and "flow" it can be good to try this with eyes almost closed!

Try doing this to music as well.

14. Collage: shape and texture

Make an image of what you have seen/done with black tissue on white paper. Tear, crumple and fold the tissue, and maybe cut it, and glue in place. Topics might be the bark of different trees, the forms out of a Shapes session, the outlines of ducks on a pool, the silhouettes of trees against the sky - or try turning it round and work in white on black to capture the sky seen through winter trees.

15. Scale

On a big piece of paper, do a very big drawing of a very small thing (a snail shell perhaps, or a passing ladybird). Then on a smaller piece of paper draw a very detailed drawing of a very small piece of a big object.

16. Texture Pictures

Working in small groups, build a picture on the ground of the most striking things you have seen/met/experienced using only things you can find around you. This does not have to be a "flat" picture: it could grow upwards as well. Try to make a "picture" that might convey its message by touch as much as by sight.

17. Bigger Pictures
Use chalks and draw along a footpath. As a whole group, do this to music and play a sort of "musical chairs" giving just a couple of minutes scribbling at any one place.

Moving on from straightforward "warm-ups", it can be very profitable to combine several short activities to make a single session that brings people together and starts their imaginations working quickly before getting on to the main business of the day. **Personal Trees** was devised by three of us (Malcolm Green, Cate Clark and myself) working together in mixed media workshops to give people a taste of the different skills they would meet and to fire their own imaginations.

PERSONAL TREES
Time: 30 - 45 minutes
Materials: sheets of paper and various coloured pencils, crayons and pastels
Organisation: involves whole group in various formats

Stage 1: The story of your tree
1. - "to talk about trees....." - trees are important, trees as landmarks of place and character, the trees of our childhood, does everyone have a tree or trees that are, or have been, important to them?
2. - in pairs - tell the story of you and your tree quietly to someone else
3. - gather everyone back together and listen to a couple of stories if people would like to share them with the company (don't listen to all of them!)

Stage 2: Drawing your tree
Take a sheet of paper and spend 5 or 10 minutes sketching quickly the shapes, the feel, the outline of your story. Perhaps add a couple of words that help sum up the whole experience for yourself.

Stage 3: Shaping your tree
Divide into groups of 4 or 5 and use **Body Sculpture** to create the feel of your tree and then fit yourself into the scene. Work through the trees of everyone in your group, sort out a sequence and then present your trees to the the rest of the company.

Enjoy everyone else's trees.

This same sequence was used with "significant moments" - environmental experiences outside of specifically tree-related ones and with "playing with nature" - memories of childhood play in adults. Some movement in the Sculpture session is useful but with "playing" there was a tendency for the still, captured moment that we were looking for to turn into lots of dashing around which did not feel quite as appropriate.

SPECTACULAR STANDARDS

Standards have been used for ages to identify peoples: rallying points in battle, a stake to claim a territory, a "name post" in the centre of a village. They have taken all manner of shapes from Roman eagles to the fluttering flag on a Cavalry lance. Standards are not necessarily martial features: your group is hopefully not about to go to war! They could just as easily be emblems carried to a great celebratory gathering of the clans so that everyone can identify everyone else.

Working with groups, the chance to make a standard can be an effective way of building a group identity and a good starting point for sharing ideas and drawing people who may not have worked together before into a joint project. The standard can become the image that declares "this is who we are".

Leaders' Notes

Aztec insignia (after Hoffman)

Materials: depends very much on the form you are taking. For those illustrated here, as well as basic kit, you would need:
branch: materials for tassles and a branch found on site; **shield:** two long poles to form a cross, material for tassles, two large cardboard discs (front and back); **Aztec:** one long pole, two large cardboard discs (or the back may be a piece of wire grid, or perforated hardboard), access to reedmace, etc.
hub-cap: strong branch or pole, found hubcaps, material for tassles

36

Time: again this depends upon what you plan, but if everyone is involved simultaneously it should not take very long.

Organisation: a group activity. You can approach making a standard with a definite time set aside to do the work but just as a group's identity takes a while to form, so can your group standard. Try organising things so that the standard can be worked on as and when individuals feel inspired while other activities are also running. If you take this approach, do make sure everyone has their chance to make their contribution to the final piece.

> "....we went on a weekend camping trip together and used the time to create a shield. We used a large wooden hoop with a circle of leather lashed to it. Because of our work with the dark and light we painted one half of it white and one black. Margie drew an owl on one half and an eagle on the other, with wings overlapping into the opposite colour.........
>
> We decided that it was time to declare a deeper level of commitment to our lodge and one another so we agreed to each tie a feather that we had decorated in a unique manner to the shield to declare that commitment. We spontaneously created a wonderful ceremony as we each added our feather........
>
> When a member leaves the circle we have a ceremony in which she removes her feather and ties a small shadow feather in its place so that her spirit energy remains present on the shield." from *The Ceremonial Circle* by Sedonia Cahill and Joshua Halpern

Hints: however you plan the activity, some points to bear in mind might include:

~ make sure everyone has their chance to contribute if they want to

~ the finished product should be striking enough to be identifiable over a distance

~ it probably needs to be fairly portable - plan for something that one, or maybe two people could carry

The possible shapes your standard could take are very varied: four suggestions are given here, but your group could go where its inspiration takes it.

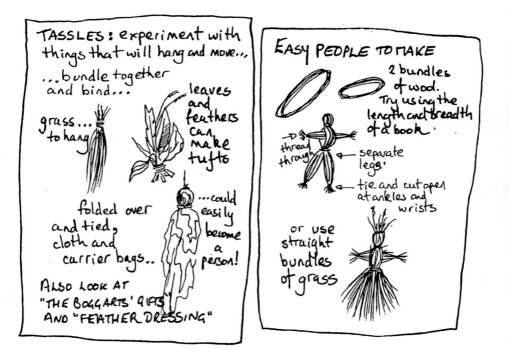

TASSLES: experiment with things that will hang and move...

...bundle together and bind...

grass... to hang

leaves and feathers can make tufts

folded over and tied, cloth and carrier bags...

...could easily become a person!

ALSO LOOK AT "THE BOGGARTS' GIFTS" AND "FEATHER DRESSING"

EASY PEOPLE TO MAKE

2 bundles of wool. Try using the length and breadth of a book.

thread through

separate legs.

tie and cut open at ankles and wrists

or use straight bundles of grass

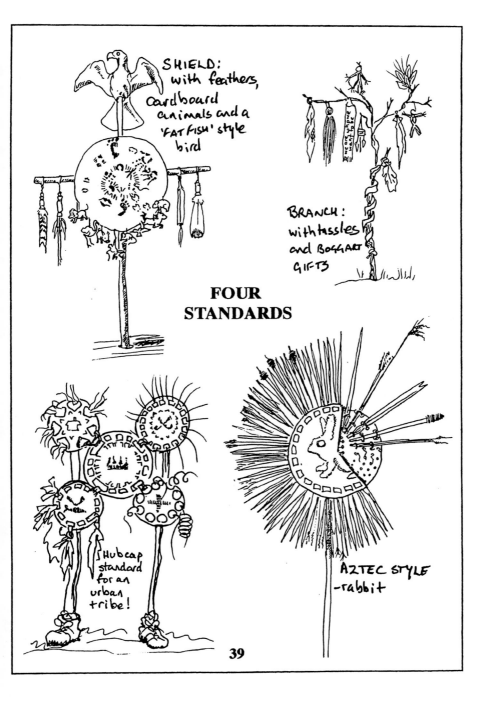

SHIELD:
with feathers,
cardboard
animals and a
'FAT FISH' style
bird

BRANCH:
with tassles
and BOGGART
GIFTS

**FOUR
STANDARDS**

Hubcap
standard
for an
urban
tribe!

AZTEC STYLE
-rabbit

39

CRAZY HATS, HAIRDOES AND HEAD SCULPTURES

An assortment of things to do on the tops of people's heads may well count as one of the silliest sets of activities in this book. And so they are - a frivolous selection, but used well they can offer people a chance to explore and interpret quite abstract concepts, weather for example, in sculptural forms.

Making hats involves catching the "essence" of a thing - grasping the vital features that make any incident, place or experience distinctive. To create "winter" on the top of your own (or someone else's) head can be an exercise in finding the colours and shapes that, at a glance, say "winter" to a stray passerby.

How these activities are fitted in with others gives them purpose without robbing them of their sense of delighted madness. Exploration and observation is always invaluable - offer your group a feast of experiences to draw upon and follow up, perhaps, with **Body Sculpture** and **Shapes** sessions to help pull ideas together before they become environmental milliners.

Leaders' Notes
CRAZY HATS
Materials: basic kit with lots of card, and coloured sugar, tissue and crepe papers

Time: 11/2 - 2 hours

Organisation: individuals, or in pairs when it is often easier to help one another to make a hat

Getting started: a good challenge to offer might be "...create a flowerbed on your head..."

Comments: this activity proved heavy on card and paper and had a tendency to be very "stylish hat" in flavour which was fine if one was aiming for a Hat Party but often felt quite a long way from the original intent. Easy to supply materials for.

HAIRDOES
Materials: basic kit with tough net or rug canvas, the netting bags that fruit or vegetables sometime come in, or stockingette from car parts supplier. Other useful bits are listed with the notes on Head Sculptures
Time: 2 hours or more for a really dense growth
Organisation: pairs was often easiest, with people helping each other to make individual pieces. **Preparation:** if you go for rug canvas caps, the pieces for these need cutting out - a slow process

Getting started: offer a challenge: perhaps show some of the wilder modern Fairy drawings (artists like Brian Froud and Alan Lee) for inspiration and work towards "...being able to kneel down in the middle of this field of grass and flowers/this undergrowth and disappear..but still to be able to watch what is going on!"
Comments: canvas caps give a good strong base to work upon but are time consuming and fidgetty to make. Tough netting laced up into a cone is a reasonable alternative. Netting bags can be easy to get but do not offer a lot of support. Among materials, "sea grass" and raffia are good for giving some body to the whole thing and unravelled sea grass gives a wonderful springy effect. Encourage people to think about movement in their hair dressing - a flock of butterflies on withy tips perhaps, bobbing above some flowers.

HEAD SCULPTURES
Materials: basic kit with extra newspaper and scrap card and "other useful bits" -see below
Time: 1 - 1.5 hours
Organisation: probably working alone, perhaps with a friend nearby to talk to, or maybe in pairs with each person helping the other as needed

Getting started: "...build your favourite weather (or season, or continent, or whatever) on your head..."

Comments: a great opportunity for a sculptural adventure here. Encourage your group to think along a number of different lines, as below. The abstract thought of it can put some people off, so it can be worth starting with hats and then gently coaxing people's hats over the edge into the more freeform shapes here

Other useful bits: sea grass, from Craft Suppliers - used in making stools and chairs; raffia - Craft and School suppliers; coloured polystyrene packing - some of the chips can be threaded onto things; bubble wrap, various colours and sizes of bubble; shredded paper packaging (check it first); feathers.

CRAZY HATS

Fasten crowns to brims with folded tabs
Make domes by making a tube the right size, cutting down from the top then folding these sections down in turn and stapling together as you go

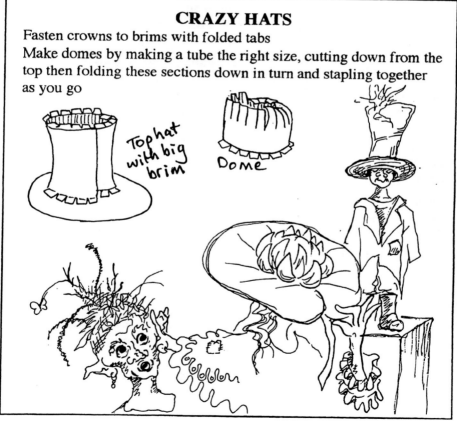

Top hat with big brim

Dome

HEAD SCULPTURES

start with a cap of
tough card and
then....

think **SHAPE** - what
simple shapes show
what you are thinking
of

cloud bundle

think **SIZE** - with
light materials you
can build something
very big

weather shapes

mist
rain
clouds
storm

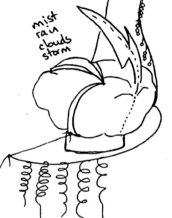

think **MOVEMENT** - try
using spirals, curls, and
curves inside your sculpture,
dangling coils, twists, fronds
and leaves could hang down
around it

think **UP, DOWN**
and **OUT** - you
have a lot of space
around you

keep **DETAILS** for last - a
parade of penguins, a single
butterfly

sun and
rainbow
on a
stick!

OTHER THINGS TO TRY
~ withy tips for height and
support
~ grass stalks to make fans
~ cut cardboard and paper to
make spirals
~ pull paper strips over a pencil
to make curls
~ tissue paper or wool waste can
give big clouds
~ leaves can be threaded onto
string or spiked on a withy for
more structure

HAIRDOES

the shape to aim for here is a cap that fits quite snugly onto your head

rug canvas - cut 2 fronts and 2 backs and fasten together by overlapping edges and lacing up with wool

or use a net onion or fruit bag

try making a cap out of garden netting

then use similar ideas to **Head Sculptures** but go as much for **movement** as for **shape**

WORKING WITH WILLOW

Willow trees are full of mixed tales in many lands. People hold very ambiguous feelings about these versatile trees. We use their wood for cricket bats and thatching spars, sheep hurdles and baskets; their bark gives a cinnamon dye, the original pain-killing "aspirin" and can tan leather; their leaves serve as autumn fodder for cattle and horses and may even be tokens of rejected love - or a distant lover. But we have seen a darker side to the golden willow - a sense of threat heard in the whispering voices of a willow wood after dark and an old promise that if you fell a tree: "Elm do grieve, oak do hate but willow will walk if you travels late".

OSIER
SALIX VIMINALIS

In both modern conservation and sculpture, willow is seeing a welcome revival. The art of coppicing is returning: stands of willow being cut on rotation, creating woodlands of standing trees surrounded by a range of thickets sprouting from the cut "stools" of other trunks. This creates a range of copses and clearings, offering a richness of habitats for a wide range of plants and animals.

All around my hat, I shall wear the green willow;
All around my hat for a twelve-month and a day;
And if anyone should ask me, the reason why I'm a'wearin' it;
It's all for my true love, who's far, far away.
Traditional

Coppiced wood grows quickly and, harvested at different ages, gives a mixture of material to work with: thicker pieces can be turned on a polelathe or become charcoal for cooking and heating (and drawing!) while the young, whip thin withies give a wonderful medium for basketry and sculpture - light, flexible, plentiful and cheap. With a bit of practice it is easy to use in creating giant shapes. If the ends are set in the ground, freshly cut stalks will even take root and whole sculptures may start sprouting. look out for growing willow figures and houses in country parks all over the country. On a smaller scale, fresh willow, or dried and bark-stripped withy make excellent frames for models, masks and lanterns.

> WILLOW
> ...Now I can love willows again, in a wild
> country. Their silver softens the hedge:
> their gold attracts early bees.
> When I touch the stems, they tremble.
> But in the wind they winnow secretly;
> and I'm wary of a power that drags at me
> as the moon drags the seas.
> The Tree Calendar, Hilary Llewellyn-Williams

Leaders' Notes

There are no real hard and fast rules here: it does take a little practice to grow accustomed to the ways of willow - how easily it bends, the sorts of shapes it lends itself most readily to. Flexibility is very variable: keep your willow damp. Freshly cut shoots should be used within a couple of days and stored somewhere cool and damp between whiles. Dry withy needs to be damped down before use or it will tend to snap. You can hose it down briefly (messy and fun); dunk it in a pond (messier and even more fun); lie it on a tarpaulin, pour a bucket of water over it and as the water drains away, cover it lightly with a fold of tarpaulin until needed (effective but not a lot of fun); or even lie it in damp grass. Have a rag handy to wipe off surface water or taping a frame together can be tricky!

WITHY FRAMES

Material: a bundle of withies - 5 or 10 each shape, scissors, string and lots of masking tape (1cm is perhaps best, or 2.5cm can always be torn down the middle for a more manageable width)

Time: very unpredictable - how complicated is the shape you want to make? To start with, give your group a couple of hours and something fairly straightforward to work with - maybe a flat butterfly or fish shape.

Organisation: people could work alone, or in pairs to start with. As experience grows, and the shapes get bigger, so can the groups.

What do you do?

Bend the withy, gently and tape it in place. That's it.

Start with the outline and use the heavier ends of the withies on the areas that need

Hints

~ have lots of short bits of tape ready
~ wipe down withy immediately before use
~ bend gently for curves
~ be careful on sharp corners
~ work with grace
~ keep looking at or thinking of the final result
~ but don't be surprised or disappointed when it turns into something else!
~ fill in details inside shapes: don't leave big open spaces
~ sing to the willow - it keeps everyone cheerful
~ have a Bug Rescue Box handy if the willow is fresh

least curvature and greatest strength. Keep the finer tips to bend and fold and fill the shape in. Tape each joint securely but do not overload on tape so that it looks all knobbly-kneed.

Finished?

You could fill the frame with more willow and go for a "basket" type finish, or weave in wool, feathers and things for an intriguing textured sculpture, or you could give the whole thing a "skin" of tissue paper.

SKINNING A FRAME

Materials: your frame, a washing up bowl, PVA glue and water (mixed 50:50, or 60:40) a bath sponge, white tissue paper, a table to work on, or a plastic tarpaulin
Time: 30 minutes for a small (1m across) piece
Organisation: this can be a very messy task: either be incredibly well-organised or minimise access to the glue bowl! To begin with, people often find it easier to work in pairs.

Start by damping down the tabletop with your glue soaked sponge: it needs to have a film of the glue-mix but shouldn't be puddled with the stuff.

Carefully lay a sheet of tissue half onto this surface and wipe down the top side. Be careful not to get the tissue too wet or it will tear. Fold the other half of the sheet onto the gluey piece and wipe down again.

Putting your sponge aside, use both hands to peel the tissue off the table by lifting it by two corners so that it hangs between your hands.

Carefully lay it on your shape.

Fold the tissue edge round withy
edges, pull it very gently to take up
the slack.

Overlap with other tissue sheets
Do not worry too much about
creases or overlaps or if the whole
thing feels a little loose: it will
tighten up as it dries and the creases
and folds add character
Use coloured tissue sparingly:
white tissue lets light through
beautifully - coloured tissue
darkens the whole thing and it is the
reaction to light that really gives
tissue/withy shapes their delight.
Try yellow or pale colours,. You
could also try sprinkling on powder paint or food colouring when the
glue is still wet. Lie the shape down (on a plastic tarpaulin) or hang it up
to dry. On a hot sunny day this may only take an hour or two, otherwise
try to leave it overnight.

LANTERNS.
Materials: withies or peasticks, masking tape, scissors, wire, jar-top,
hammer and nail (to punch a hole in the
top) candle, matches, tissue paper, bowl,
sponge, glue and water mix

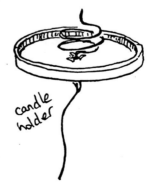

candle
holder

Time: you should be able to get a simple
pyramid lantern done in an hour
Organisation: as above - maybe start with
pairs.
If you want to make a lantern rather than a
flat shape, follow the same procedure as
above but make your frame 3 dimensional:
to start with, try making sort-of straight-
sided geometric shapes - you could even use pea-sticks for more

precision if you wanted to.

Before skinning the frame, add a candle holder in the middle of the bottom face of the figure: a metal jar-top with a hole and a coil of wire can become candle-holder and wax collector.

When the skin has dried cut a small "door" big enough to get a hand in to sort out the candle and cut a couple of smoke holes in the top. Add a loop of wire to hang the lantern by and off you go.

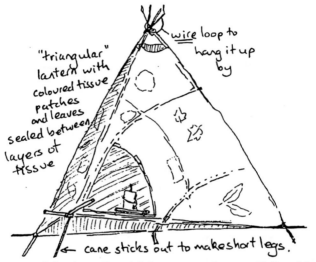

"triangular" lantern with coloured tissue patches and leaves sealed between layers of tissue

wire loop to hang it up by

← cane sticks out to makeshort legs.

Candles are surprisingly safe with lanterns when well fixed but if you are concerned about fire risks, try lighting lanterns with a light-weight "pen-light" torch.

Flat withy shapes are delightful in bright light and being light and easy to carry they naturally seem to reach up, high above people's heads: with withy shapes you can watch a giant flower-meadow lift up and come sailing across the lawn towards you. Lantern processions are wonderful things: walk your lanterns round the edge of a lake or along a canal or river and enjoy the reflections, stand in circles and admire the warm glow of gentle light.

MAPSTICKS AND TOKENS

In our world, we tend to record events as written words: diaries, letters, accounts in exercise books; increasingly we even hang onto precise recordings as photographs or video. We seem to be moving away from remembering significant moments for their meaning and the impressions they leave, towards hanging onto a picture of the event itself.

In other cultures, that pin-point accuracy is often less important than the change a situation heralds and the long-term consequences for an individual's life. A naming ceremony may, for example, identify and place a person within their community and connects them to a whole lineage of spiritual and cultural associations and obligations. The enduring feature of such an event is not the moment itself (we might keep a baptism photograph) but the connection that is made, a link that may last the rest of a person's life.

Recording such situations in a non-literate culture can take place in many ways - as songs or stories, dances, drawings or tokens. Here, we shall draw upon the idea that takes an incident, large or small and turns it into a "thing" - a "medicine object", or just "medicine", in Native American parlance. Here, colour, shape, materials and texture can all encompass

Bear Medicine: Blackfoot, North America

51

meaning - all contribute to the message contained within a shaped and structured artifact.

This could be anything from a simple carved animal totem bound to a stone, to a protective beaded tortoise to hold a child's umbilical cord, to a full scale totem pole displaying the ancestors and spirit guides of a clan.

Intriguing and exciting objects in themselves, these are also memory triggers and are very personal. Herein lies a lot of the strength of medicine objects for environmental education. We are unlikely, perhaps, to start dealing with newborn infants, or major rites of passage, but we can take the idea of capturing a moment and using it to help people absorb and interpret their environmental experiences anew.

Moving right away from the written word, a medicine object tells a story to the person who made it, and to other people only through that first individual. As long as they know the what and why of the imagery bound into the object, that can be as abstract and symbolic as the maker chooses. Artifacts can be simple in their construction as in the Charm activity described below or more complex and holding a much stronger "storyline" as the central activity in this chapter, Mapsticks, does. Power lies in the totally personal interpretation of nature and the individual ownership and understanding of the message so contained.

Leaders' Notes
A CHARM
Materials: minimal - twine and scissors are helpful to carry with you.
Time: anything from a few minutes to half an hour
Organisation: the whole company could be engaged in making their own charms or even just a single person. Where possible, it is probably better to let people spread out and find their own places to stop and reflect and enjoy a bit of peace and quiet.

MAPSTICKS - Mapsticks came about as an activity "to see what's in between". A session would start with discussion about journeys and memories of journeys and maps as ways of remembering what a journey contained...

Materials: lots of scissors, wide range of colours of wool, rolled into a number of small balls (rather than leaving it as several large balls)
Time: at least 1.5 hours for exploration and then making a mapstick, allow 2 hours+ for a relaxed session with time for talking and sharing stories at the end.
Organisation: small groups to explore the site, then the whole company together to make the mapsticks.
Getting started: *"The most important reason for going from one place to another is to see what's in between"* Norton Juster, The Phantom Tolbooth. Think about maps, and journeys - what do they mean to us, as a society and as individuals? what shapes can we record our travels in
Sequence
1. Exploring: let your company explore the site to be mapped. Small groups are probably best, perhaps each with an adult in attendance. The aim is to get to know the place, find the juicy bits, the exciting bits, the places they'd like to take someone else to. Send groups off in different directions, and arrange to meet up again after half an hour or so, During the travelling, encourage people to collect mementoes of their journey and to find an attractive stick that will form the base of their map.
2. Making: trying to make mapsticks as you travel usually results in odd wool-trails scattered across the area. At an established meeting place, people can sit down as they arrive, sort out their finds, and start binding wool and objects together onto their chosen stick (see worksheet).
3. Afterwards: a mapstick is a personal record of a journey but to be most effective, it needs to be shared. Initially, simply encourage individuals to sit down with someone from a different journey and swap stories: rotate, mingle, let people get to know the whole site through each other's eyes.

People could lead each other across the site on mapstick guided tours, or return to class and have a whole site mapped on a wall: but mapped in a three dimensional, story based interpretation rather than a flat diagrammatic representation.

Overall, however, the power of a mapstick lies in the personal ownership it gives the individual: this is their story to share if they will, their colourful, personal and special record of a visit. No-one else will ever have another the same as it.

Variations: "mapsticks" do not only have to record journeys in space, they could just as easily measure an individual's change through time - "my life", perhaps - or "what do I remember?" or "what is important to me ?"

    "stains": an interesting development can come when more time is available and rather than using wool, strip the chosen twigs of their bark and prepare stains, or paints from natural materials to colour the wood itself. This open up opportunites for working with a range of materials and inventing techniques to prepare colours from plants, earth, clay, ash and so on. Be alert for potentially dangerous sources here!

Songlines: and if you are feeling wildly adventurous take mapsticks and move onto music by turning the mapsticks into songlines.

PRAYER ARROWS - the same idea we met in Mapsticks is used in making "Prayer" or "Wishing" Arrows - that a thought may be turned into colour and pattern rather than words or pictures. Unlike the recording of a Mapstick, a Prayer Arrow sends a message to the world around us.

 Materials: 1 peastick each (25 - 30 cm long), assorted coloured wools, scissors, feathers - both long ones and small "fluffs".
Time : 30 mins
Organisation: an activity for individuals

In many cultures, birds are messengers who cross the gulf between Earth and Sky, linking all of us earthbound people with the Spirits of the heavens. Think of Christian doves and the ravens who fed Elijah in the wilderness. In American Indian myth, eagles fly the highest of all birds and prayers sent by an eagle feather fly straight to the sky. By association, a bird's feathers will also act as "transmitters" and when our Prayer Arrows stand upright in the ground and their feathers tremble and flutter in the wind, the dreams bound onto the shaft fly up and out into the air. Just as we now know that a pollutant released in one land can eventually flow along the air currents to touch all the world, so the dreams released from Prayer Arrows spread out and we can share them with people we may never meet.

Hints: - bind wool tightly to include stray ends, getting the smoothest finish possible.
   - avoid suggestions of firing the arrows! Traditionally, something like this would probably be fired and left to stand where it landed - since we may want to take ours away, they should not be launched but held close and stood upright in some special personal place.

SONGLINES - making a mapstick takes us one step away from writing and the maps we are used to. But consider: in a nomadic culture with no animals to help carry loads, any item not absolutely necessary becomes a luxury and would probably be left behind. Now, the people need still other ways of remembering their journeys and one way is to tell them. We remember things most readily when they are in some sort of a rhythm.

Materials: none, but access to stones, sticks, grass helps
Time: 1.5 hours with warm-up and performance
Organisation: warm-up activities could be done with the whole company and then work in groups of 4 - 6 people who all shared similar journeys for building the Songlines

A CHARM

  Try stopping at a key point on a walk - a nice view, a
quiet bank, the local waterfall. Choose somewhere to
rest, rummage and reflect. There collect a couple of
objects that will remind you of the occasion. If these
are bound together they can become a Charm to carry
away - this moment in miniature - to wear in one's hair,
or to add collectively to a hoop as a group impression
of the event, or simply to leave behind as a "thank-you"
to the place itself.

Rook feather, grass, wool and baler twine

MAKING A TOKEN.

"I took some of her (a pony's) tail for the wolf doll, then wandered around in the fog for the rest of the day. I scratched around in the dirt and climbed the trees, looking for feathers, pieces of bark, pieces of fur, anything unusual and appropriate. I discovered a fairly soft piece of wood by Dead Man's Creek, one that vaguely suggested a wolf body on four legs...I took bits of sage, fur and other things I scrounged, and made a lightning bundle. I wrapped it onto the belly of the wolf. The horsehair served as the tail, and I carved symbols of the night-eagle (owl) and bear onto its back. I had found glue and pieces of broken mirror in Agnes' cabin, and I glued pieces of broken shell in the mouth for snarling teeth and two pieces of the mirror above for eyes. I crushed some red berries and rubbed the wolf with the juice which looked like blood. The bird nails worked well as claws. I found myself singing a strange song as I worked - I had been singing it over and over before I realized it. It was a dream song for me."

....making a wolf doll token, from *Medicine Woman* by Lynn Andrews, Routledge, Kegan, Paul 1984.

A MAPSTICK, part 1

The journey

My journey began by a pond of cool, clear water with rushes growing around it *(blue wool with plaited rushes making a pond shape)*

Leaving the pond, I followed a path across a field. I liked this section and even though the distance was quite short, I spent a long time here *(green wool with grass stalks and leaves woven into it)*

Moving on, I walked over bare earth in a wood of alder and birch trees. There were holes among the tree-roots where I found a rabbit bone *(brown and black wool, alder cones, birch leaves)*

Making the mapstick

1. When wrapping, **keep the wool tight,** feeding one colour into the next so no unexplained bits of twig are exposed.

2. Don't start at the very bottom or work right to the very tip. A bare base gives space to thrust the finished mapstick into the ground for a useful display style, and if you work right to the end, does that mean you have finished your journey and you have nowhere else to go? At all? Do journeys ever end?

A MAPSTICK, part 2

At the end of my walk, I came out onto a field with out a path and there I stopped *(green wool with grass woven into it)*

This walk was in the early morning - the sky was clear and blue, birds were singing and the sun was rising *(pale blue wool, feathers and an orange and yellow "sun" weaving)*

3. Keep talking (if only to yourself). Everything that goes onto the stick is part of the story of your journey. Talking helps you tie object, colour and incident together.

4. Be adventurous. **Think about colour** - wool may reflect changing colours in the environment, the skies, how you feel. Create **shapes** out of things you have found: ponds woven from their rushes, a boardwalk of cracked birch twigs, a five-bar gate.

5. Special items could be added out-of-sequence to show their importance: a single wellington boot turned up on one occasion.

59

MAKING A PRAYER ARROW

On the shaft of a Prayer Arrow, we can bind any hope, or dream, or pleasure we would like to share with the rest of the world. Within a group, the thoughts that individuals want to share can be very varied and unpredictable: the night sky, my favourite animals, the Earth, flowers - there is no telling just what joy is going to be "broadcast".

Hints: - bind wool tightly to include stray ends, getting the smoothest finish possible.

- do not fire your arrow! Traditionally, something like this **would** probably be fired and left to stand where it landed -but in our crowded world this can be dangerous and since we may want to take our arrows away, they should not be launched but held onto and stood upright in some special personal place.

SOME PRAYER ARROWS

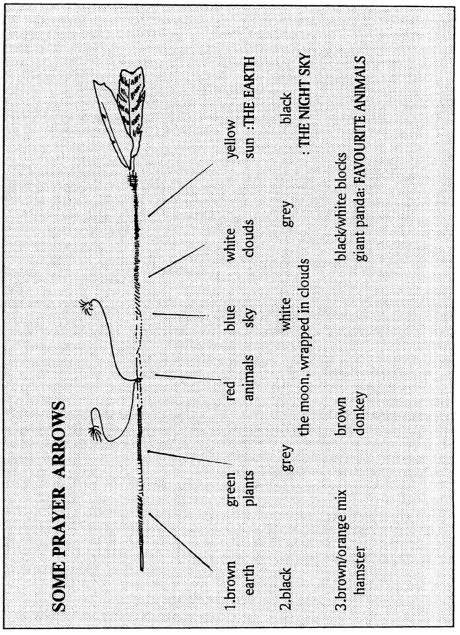

1.brown   green   red   blue   white   yellow
   earth   plants   animals sky   clouds   sun :THE EARTH

2.black   grey   white   grey   black
                       the moon, wrapped in clouds   : THE NIGHT SKY

3.brown/orange mix   brown   black/white blocks
   hamster   donkey   giant panda: FAVOURITE ANIMALS

SONGLINES

The Australian Aborigines have turned their journeys into songs. Using "Songlines", they can trace their way across huge expanses of desert, finding water, food and shelter from the information in their songs. Songlines are inherited journeys - different songs belong to different families and as well as having lots of up to date information, the stories the songs contain also explain how that stretch of land was shaped long ago when the Dreamtime Ancestors were awake and walking across the country. So, an Aboriginal Songline gives people both "physical" and "spiritual" maps of the land they live on.

We may not have the myths that shape our land available (but see **Story shields** and the **Beavers, Crows and Mosquitoes** workshop later), but we can still take our Mapsticks and learn to sing our way across the land.

This process needs leaders to be very careful: songlines can be wonderfully, wildly creative or can degenerate into doggerel versions of familiar tunes. Usually the latter happens when an adult gets closely involved with a particular group and imposes their perceptions of rhythm and rhyme upon the activity. Sometimes this will be needed but on the whole our input is very delicate: nudges, suggestions, a touch of technique and diplomacy and only stepping in more strongly as a last resort.Because Songlines need careful guidance to grow, a single worksheet has not been produced - it really depends upon a leader feeding in ideas from one stage to the next.

Activity 1: what rhymes or poems do children use regularly - skipping songs, advert jingles, counting games?.

Warming up: start by playing some easy rhythm games with the whole group - any clapping/clicking/slapping games are good: a few are included in **Move it!** Or you might like to try:

62

Activity 2: Sounds of the Land: sets of sounds derived from Native Australian rhythms.
Divide the company into 4 groups, and then...

Everyone: constant, steady count of four, stamped with the feet - keep this quite slow - count "one...and...two...and..."

Group 1 will clap in time with the footsteps - and the footsteps are the sound of the constant unchanging land.
Group 2 will click fingers or tongues on the off-beat ("...and...")
Group 3 will do a short sharp double-clap on counts 2 and 4.
Group 4 will do a very quick treble clap on count 3 (this is the trickiest one to get!).

Groups 2, 3 and 4 are all the sounds of living things who come and go and are very fleeting presences on top of the land.
And finally, when all that is going, encourage people to hum, or drone gently underneath all these other sounds - the sound of the didgeridu coming in as the Dreaming - the magic that flows through everything else.
This takes practice but is lovely when it works!

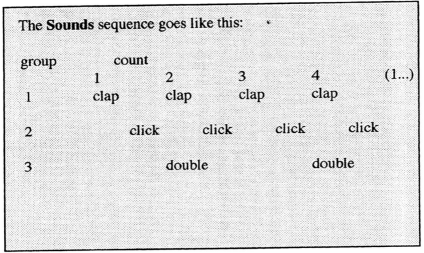

The **Sounds** sequence goes like this:

group	count 1	2	3	4	(1...)
1	clap	clap	clap	clap	
2		click	click	click	click
3		double		double	

BUILDING YOUR SONGLINES

1. Talk to each other and share the various journeys - find common points or stages and any particularly important bits.

2. Lay down the base: a solid, slightly uneven beat gives a good "footstep" feel to start with: ONE-two, ONE-two. Try it with clapping or stamping. Vary it as the journey progresses, abandon it for voice noises if needed -squelching through mud perhaps.

3. Build up layers: on top of the movement of the foundation play with words, sounds, improvised instruments to add appropriate layers of incident to the journey. Words can be used singly or repeated as individual words or phrases to form little asides or longer chants. Use the local environment as a source of sound effects and simple instruments - but do keep it simple, a full orchestra is as inappropriate here as a road atlas!

4. Don't get too complicated or it may all crumble into stage-fright when everyone assembles to sing their new Songlines to each other.

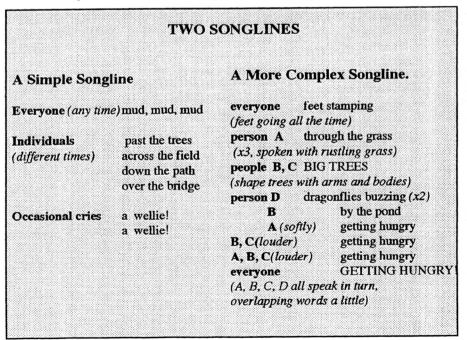

TWO SONGLINES

A Simple Songline

Everyone *(any time)*	mud, mud, mud
Individuals *(different times)*	past the trees across the field down the path over the bridge
Occasional cries	a wellie! a wellie!

A More Complex Songline.

everyone	feet stamping
(feet going all the time)	
person A	through the grass
(x3, spoken with rustling grass)	
people B, C	BIG TREES
(shape trees with arms and bodies)	
person D	dragonflies buzzing *(x2)*
B	by the pond
A *(softly)*	getting hungry
B, C *(louder)*	getting hungry
A, B, C *(louder)*	getting hungry
everyone	GETTING HUNGRY

(A, B, C, D all speak in turn, overlapping words a little)

THE BOGGARTS' GIFTS

Boggarts are people of the world of Faerie - that strange, wild, reckless place that lies behind the enchantment of lonely moors and silent woodlands and speaks in the wind that rustles the leaves of autumn. The relationships between humans and Faeries are the stuff of countless folktales and the best way to get any feel of that is to tell some of these stories and laugh and wonder and groan in dismay at the ups and downs of coping with non-human neighbours.

> "They avoid looking smart, and well dressed, apart from Hob Headless, and are easily insulted, especially by offers of new clothes, or a wash and tidy. They're quick to change their moods - noisy, proud, loud and boastful, silent and sulky, loving enthusiastic, sentimental and over-excited. They have a tendency to talk all together all at once when they're trying to discuss something, and in general are more like us than we are ourselves. Boggarts are elemental creatures, and have special and magical qualities according to their kind. They can all manage to be invisible sometimes - though some find it easier than others. " from *Boggart Sandwich* by Martin Riley

The people of Faerie come in a bewildering array of shapes and sizes - and colour, and textures and smells - from the dazzling beauty of the noble Daoine Sidhe of Ireland and Scotland to the Cornish Muryans (doomed to get smaller with each generation until they finally disappear). Boggarts stumble into this array somewhere between the kitchen fireplace and the edge of the wildwood, with "boggart" as a handy term for a range of people from Scottish Brownies and Gruagachs, to the household Hobs of Oxfordshire, Fenodyree from the Isle of Man and assorted bogles from all over the place.

They are volatile, quick to anger and to joy, reward diligence and hard work but pinch the calves of laziness, and are not above sneezing the soot from up the chimney all over the living room carpet. Some stories, however, pick out a subtler seasonal pattern than simply that of trouble-some home- and farm-helps. " They (people) thought as the earth was sleeping all the Winter; and that the bogles...had nobbut to do but mis-chief, for they'd nowt to see to in the fields.....But as the Winter went by, they thought as it were time to wake the earth from its sleeping and set the bogles to work, caring for the growing things, and bringing the harvest." (Alan Garner, *Book of British Fairy Tales*).

Traditional stories are a wonderful way of drawing people into the magic of their own places - most parts of the country have their own "fairy stories" that spin from tales of everyday encounters with the improbable to full scale
earth-shaping myths of the origins of hills and mountains, the depths of lakes and the flow of rivers. Looking at the world from a Boggart per-spective is a good way of breaking conventional imagery and approach-ing the familiar with an inspired imagination.

The Boggarts' Gifts come from a workshop "The Boggarts at Midwin-ter" which is described later. Together with these go **Festive Goblins**, which came as a challenge to shape your own boggart out of leaves and wildness and hang a bit of the untamed, everyday countryside among all the other decorations at Christmas. These lead, almost inevitably, to work with animation and setting your boggarts to dancing, but that can come with another chapter.

Leaders' Notes
THE BOGGARTS' GIFTS - These are a variety of decorations to hang on a tree, branch, earlobe or whatever. Fashioned out of scrap and found

materials, make the most of the colours and textures to be found in the small things of winter. The first four activities are all quite short but the Dangly Wotsits are more fiddly although very rewarding and the rag poems are an effective quick end to other **wordstuff** activities.

Materials: basic kit, strong thread or button twine and needles, calico, garden netting, scrap card, double-sided tape and access to a mixture of leaves, roots, twigs, etc.
Time: 30 mins, or less, sees most of these through
Organisation: good activities for small groups, each person making their own decoration but sharing resources and boggarty conversation

FESTIVE GOBLINS - a cheerful and friendly activity that produces lively results.
Materials: twine, modelling clay (plasticine or flour and water), scissors, leaves, roots, twigs, etc
Time: 20 minutes or so - more if you spend a lot of time looking for bits to use
Organisation: for individuals, but an easy activity for a whole class to be engaged in. Festive Goblins can come out of other explorations of a site - collect material as you go, or could be used as a small session in its own right.

THE BOGGARTS' GIFTS, part 1

Trees: cut two triangles of packing box card - cut so that the internal corrugations run vertically through the shapes. Decorate the surfaces, slash and slot the

triangles together then slide exciting things into the sides of the triangles

Stones: same procedure as with Trees but work with oval shapes and decorate with pictures of the shapes, colours and animals of winter earth. Nice opportunities here for showing grass stalks and the vein networks of roots

Stars: 8 - 10cm disc of card with double-sided sticky-tape on both sides: peel off the tape and get to work!

Tinsel: use a metre long thin piece of garden netting and weave into this almost anything that is not too completely revolting, or wriggles to make a strip of "tinsel" straight from the bottom of a pond

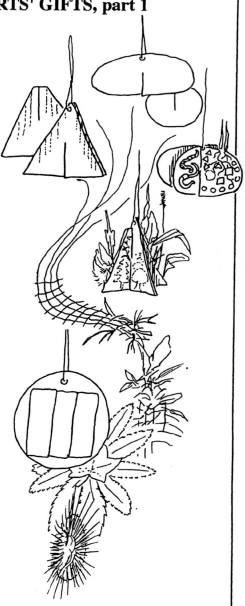

THE BOGGARTS' GIFTS, part 2

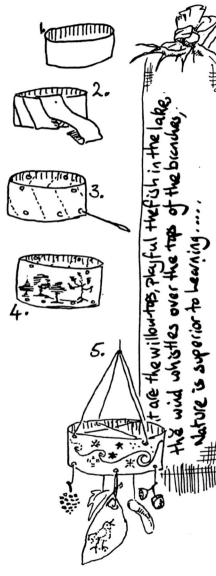

Dangly Wotsits: 1. Cut a 2cm or so broad section from a cardboard tube. 2. If you want, wrap this around with masking tape for strength - this is, however, a harder surface to draw on. 3. Carefully, pierce 4 holes along the upper edge and 6 or so round the lower. 4. Decorate the whole band - perhaps pictures of your winter experiences? 5. Thread button twine through the top holes to make a hanging loop and suspend interesting bits and bobs from the lower holes. Dry leaves, feathers and flakes of bark could all be drawn on as well. There is a trick to balancing all these bits, so enjoy it!

Rag Poems: take a strip of calico, or other lightweight plain cloth, perhaps 40cm long and 8cm or so wide. Slash one end about 10cm along the centre. Send a message to the world with a pen, pencil or piece of charcoal along the remaining cloth and tie it to hang from the branches of your own "Clootie Tree".

FESTIVE GOBLINS

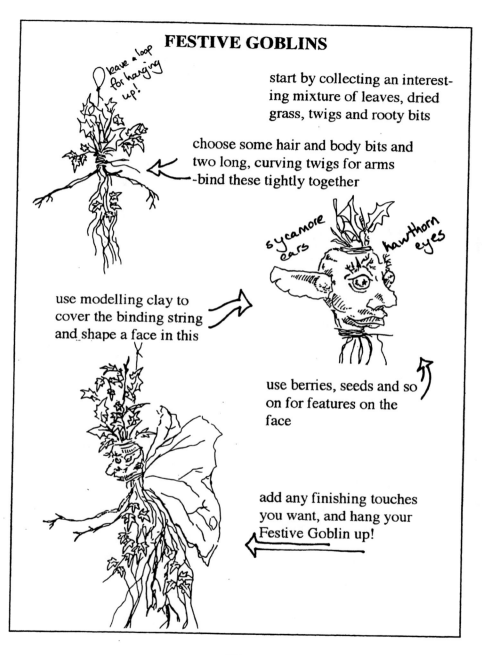

leave a loop for hanging up!

start by collecting an interesting mixture of leaves, dried grass, twigs and rooty bits

choose some hair and body bits and two long, curving twigs for arms -bind these tightly together

sycamore ears

hawthorn eyes

use modelling clay to cover the binding string and shape a face in this

use berries, seeds and so on for features on the face

add any finishing touches you want, and hang your Festive Goblin up!

THE MIDWINTER BOGGARTS

A one day workshop taking the idea of boggarts as spirits of nature, busy during spring and summer but sinking to sleep in autumn and over winter. This year, however, they are disturbed and wake in December to find all the glamour and excitement of midwinter and the festive season. Never to be outdone, the boggarts set out to explore this idea of "celebration when everything seems dead" and have their own Midwinter Party.

The workshop stayed very carefully within frivolous and seasonal limits - we were exploring the nature of the midwinter season and something of what humans get up to. We avoided unleashing boggart perceptions upon the religious background to Christmas. An underlying desire for celebration at this darkest time of the year and the need to watch out for the sun during these longest of nights, arose out of the children's own reflections on the season, letting them shape their own interpretations of the turning wheel of the seasons and lending another layer of awareness to the final performances.

Format:

    story: a good boggart tale of silliness and folly to get us all going, introduce the idea of what boggarts are, where you might find them, and what would they think of a modern December?

    invent-a-boggart: body sculpture in groups to shape a boggart out of your imagination - show the place where the boggart lives and the boggart within it. This produced under-the-bridge boggarts, cake tin boggarts (who always eat the last piece), hay field boggarts, muddy puddle boggarts and more....

    winter: small group brainstorms - impressions of the season

    the boggart dance: a created parade with lots of stamping and arm-waving and sudden wary stillness - we used a piece of music called "Trixi" by Lene Lovich

    walk: a walk into winter using environmental awareness activities to explore the changing seasons, thoughts of weather, impressions and the like

life in winter? different groups now look at ponds, grass, hedgerows and stones in more depth - each group also works a poem of their place

shaping winter: those groups now become the boggarts of the various habitats and work together to make boggart decorations inspired by those habitats, use their poem to create a performance piece with body sculpture and words, and throw in anything else that reflects their boggart perceptions of their homes at this time of year.

Finale: the boggarts gather for the boggart dance, parade their gifts (suspended from dried knotweed stalks and then assembled in a large bucket), present their own interpretations of winter with words and movements and end with a quiet story of stillness and a final dance.

"one leg up
one leg down
hang onto
next boggart
and wave
yourself
about!"

WORDSTUFF

Words are wonderfully powerful little things - they let us do so much and offer us such acres of excitement to play with. They describe our experience of the world so completely it seems: pens like paintbrushes of experience and image rather than just colours.

Here our aim is to encourage people to enjoy language. Not to worry about spelling and grammar and stuff like that but to revel in the richness of words and feel comfortable about using them: every word could be a gem that can stand alone or that we can build whole necklaces out of.
The activities here are presented as a set of stages but do not need to be followed as such - the various components of Stage 1 certainly fit comfortably in with other activities as ways of gathering images, impressions and feelings during other work.
This chapter, like the others, is about short activities: it cannot address the range of skills called for in story-telling or do more than touch upon the delights of writing poetry: try the books in the relevant section of the Bibliography for that.

STAGE ONE: gathering images
1. Somewhere special...
Time: anything from 10- 20 minutes (or more)
Materials: pencil and piece of card for everyone
Organisation: an activity for individuals - maybe stay in pairs but collect own words rather than a partner's.

Sit somewhere that appeals and take time to stop and enjoy it. Write down a word or phrase that tells how each sense responds to the place....
close your eyes and open them....what colours meet you?
sit with eyes closed and listen....name the sounds, describe a sound
breathe deeply.....think about temperature and smell
stick your tongue out....like a snake taste the air, snow on your tongue's

tip, the temperature
feel....the ground beneath you, the tree beside you, enjoy textures
Write these down, or just remember them.

2. Dreaming

Time: 10 - 20 minutes - sometimes takes a bit of time to get going and
you may need to encourage or prompt initially
Materials: usually nothing, or maybe an object to "Dream" around
Organisation: work in groups of 5 or 6 -
or more when people are used to listening.
Indoors a slightly darkened room helps the
concentration. Sometimes it helps to have
a "speaking stick" to pass round so that
each person knows when their turn to
speak comes and the group as a whole is
encouraged to respect the right of the
speaker to have their uninterrupted attention. (A speaking stick can be a decorated
stick or even just a round stone). Alternatively, the "right to speak" might simply be
passed with a touch. To end the cycle, you
might ask people to stop after a certain
number of rounds - after 3 or 4, ideas are
usually coming more freely, or simply call
a halt. Or you could let a cycle run on, but

a speaking stick

as individuals decide they do not want to speak, they fill their "speaking
space" with silence and when all the circle is silent the Dreaming is over.

Sit in a close circle and think of the space in the middle of your group as
an empty bowl, perhaps, or a still, dark pool. It helps to close your eyes
to shape the pictures people's words create. As each person speaks,
think of the image their words creates in your head start to fill up that
bowl or float across the pool. Don't try to analyse or examine, just let
their words give you pictures...

Dreaming One: from one starting point e.g. "autumn" each person drops in a single word or phrase that captures some aspect of that theme for them.

Dreaming Two: still with a single theme, let each speaker's image inspire the next person so that a string of images spirals outwards and often takes unexpected directions.

Dreaming Three: use a theme that changes, moving on after each round - stages in a lifecycle might be a good one here, or seasons again.

3.Quick stories
There are lots of story techniques to explore but here is one that can quickly get imaginations going. While this sort of activity might not always seem to have a direct relation to other activities, it can be a very good way of warming imaginations up and getting people reaching out into the unexpected corners of their thoughts.

Materials: an interesting object for each group - my box of goodies contains a large shell, a bone, a model mouse, a small dragon, a pottery walnut with a face peering out of it, a peacock feather, a frond from a tree fern, a fossil, a small African gourd cup
Time: 20 minutes
Organisation: work in groups of five or six

Offer each group an object, a thing, a treasure that can tell its own special story - every story is unique, wonderful and exciting and it is up to them to tell it. Each person can spin a sentence or two of the whole tale (watch out for the talkative ones who can dominate the whole event), carrying the narrative from where the last person left it up to a point where they say "....and then...." - the next person takes over.
You may need to encourage a starting point: "Once upon a time, a walnut fell out of an oak tree.....". A useful ending can be to take the object through to its arrival in the hands of the group. Allow time to let each group tell its story back to the rest of the class.

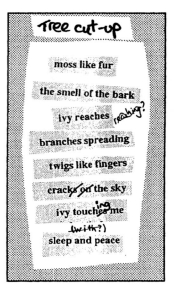

"once there was a wooden cup..."

---and a kingfisher caught fish in it, and then... he used it as a pot to cook the fish, and then... he used it as a spoon to eat the fish, and then... the kingfishers made their nest in it and laid eggs, and,....

STAGE TWO: putting it together

Once your company has started gathering ideas and images from the world around them, you can start building these into stronger and wider expressions of their feelings. Playing with rhythm can help here. Working with the way words sound and how they fit together to make comfortable shapes can create whole written or spoken pieces freed from the dangers of doggerel that can easily infect things if we try to work recklessly with rhyme.

4. Stories

Tell traditional stories and listen to the way a good story has its own rhythm. Feel the way things grow and settle and build up again. Listen for the places where a story-teller draws responses from her audience. Try "The Dead Moon" by Kevin Crossley-Holland for some very atmospheric tales from East Anglia.

5. Cut-ups

Materials: scissors, paper, pencil
Time: 15 minutes
Organisation: work as individuals or maybe in pairs
Take the words or phrases collected in **Somewhere Special** (individual or pairs) or a **Dreaming** (the group) and write them down in a list if you haven't already done so. Cut out each word or phrase and start rearranging them.

Tree cut-up

moss like fur

the smell of the bark

ivy reaches (reaching?)

branches spreading

twigs like fingers

cracks for the sky

ivy touches me (ing)

sleep and peace (with?)

76

Experiment until the whole thing "sounds right".

Taking this further, a few small words could be added: and, the, is, are and so on but nothing major! - to help it flow more smoothly. Practice together and then perform the piece - with actions if need be!

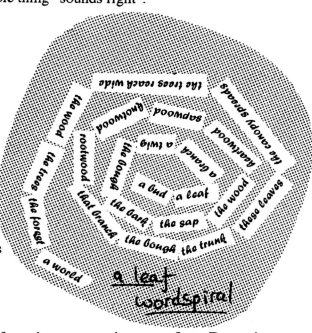

6. Wordspirals
Materials: paper, pencils
Time: 15 - 20 minutes
Organisation: pairs, individuals or small groups!

Working from the sorts of word sequences that come from **Dreaming Two** record these in a pattern. One of the simplest and most effective is to start in the middle of a piece of paper with the first word and then simply spiral the others in sequence out from it.

This can be a satisfying way of recording impressions - it manages to hold onto something of the excitement of the feelings that simply listing "what we said" loses. A group does not need to work with spirals - they could be encouraged to create shapes that reflect the object under discussion. Think of the shapes that leaves, spiders, wind or weather might offer. If the resources are available, another variation is to create the pattern in felt-tip pens on acetate sheets and stick these on the windows of a room to keep returning to for inspiration.

HAIKU

Haiku are a long established form of Japanese poetry where, in just a few lines and syllables, the reader is given an image and a thought. Their very brevity adds to their impact - every word is measured for the weight it carries. A lot of traditional Haiku follow very strict rules of line and syllable (try working your words into exactly 17 syllables for a useful word discipline exercise) but the great Haiku poet Basho started the "Soun" or free verse school of Haiku particularly for Haiku on natural topics. Soun Haiku is just as potent in its impact as more formal styles and may be even shorter and more striking than others.

Try these:
> *On the dead limb*
> *Squats a crow -*
> *Autumn night.*

> *Sparrows*
> *In the rape-field,*
> *Blossom-viewing.*

Think of Haiku as having three sections:

    1. The situation or condition you are observing - a moment caught in a phrase:
> *Wake, butterfly -*

    2. A pause, a breath to absorb the image, marked by " - "or " , "

    3. A thought or perception coming out of the observation of 1:
> *it's late, we've miles*
> *to go together*

Keep words short and language simple.

Go for clear images.

(Haiku from *Of love and barley: Haiku of Basho*)

7. More words

Materials: paper, pencils
Time: 20 - 30 minutes
Organisation: individuals or pairs

Preparation: find poems that offer you something of the feelings you would like your group to capture from their own place. Perhaps use some of the image activities above to start ideas going, and then let people play with the words.

The emphasis here is on listening to the rhythm of the piece: that matching syllables or repeating certain key words creates an atmosphere all of its own that, with care and simple vocabulary, can carry a great weight with listeners. (Look at the Leaf Wordspiral above)
Try:
> matching the first words or phrases
> matching syllables in a line: in pairs, fours, alternate lines
> keeping language and imagery simple
> writing **Haiku**

Here are some examples:

> *Keen the wind,*
> *Bare the hill,*
> *It is difficult to find shelter*
> *The ford is marred,*
> *The lake freezes,*
> *A man could stand on a single stalk*

Speak this out loud and listen to the rhythm in it. Like a Dreaming offers successions of images to build a total picture - you could try adding some more lines to complete that picture.

Or:

Snow falls, white the surface...
Snow falls, white the hoarfrost...
Snow falls, on the top of the ice...
Snow falls, it covers the valley.....

These are from traditional Celtic pieces, parts of much bigger poems, but in these "distilled" versions we can feel the atmosphere the bard would have created with his words.

Try speaking this modern poem and listen to the sounds of the words themselves....

Come will the quick, come,
Come will the dead, come,
Come will my killer, come
Come!
Come will the peat, come,
Come will the kale, come
Come will the kine, come
Come!

Come will the wings, come,
Wings cutting air,
Come will the waves, come,
Foam upon the shingle!

Come will the tree, come
Holy thorn, twisted tree,
Come will the storm, come,
Through the bruised sky screaming!

Come will the Height, come
Come will the Depth, come,
Come will the Quarters, come
Come will the Centre, come,
Come will the Flame, come
Come will the Dark, come
Come will the Wild, come
Come will the Free, come
Come will my Family, come
Come will we all,come
Together, once again!

This is part of a shaman's summoning song for earth-spirits. Find the rhythm in it and try saying it alone, with instruments, in groups and in rounds.

STAGE THREE: bigger pieces

So far, activities here have explored images and started working with rhythm and hopefully got people enjoying the words themselves as in other places we may delight in the paints on a palette. A final step, to really bind inspiration with place is to work on a person's own "identification" chant.

8.Identification Poems

Materials: paper, pencils
Time: up to an hour
Organisation: this activity needs to come out of earlier ones with ideas building up to be given a final shape in a poem or chant. It can either work as small groups pooling ideas to create a group piece or individuals working on their own poems with perhaps a friend to bounce ideas off. Encourage the use of rhythm makers (anything from sticks, stones and feet to drums and bells) and try to end the session with a performance of finished pieces.

Irish stories tell of the arrival of the Celts: the Sons of Mil, who were repulsed when they tried to land on Ireland, confused and defeated by the magic of the People of Dea who lived there at that time. But the Chief Druid of the Celts, Amergin, stood up in his boat and sang the following song. One interpretation of the Song of Amergin is that with these words he claimed a relationship with the land his people hoped to colonise - Amergin recognises his people's place in the local ecology - and by this they could assert the right to live and belong there.

Speak Amergin's Song (it loses some of its shape in translation) and then use your work with images, shapes and rhythms with your group to help them build their own Songs that link People to Place.....

I am the wind on the sea;
I am the wave of the sea;
I am the bull of seven battles;
I am the eagle on the rock;
I am a flash from the sun;
I am the most beautiful of plants;
I am a strong wild boar;
I am a salmon in the water;
I am a lake in the plain;
I am the word of knowledge;
I am the head of the spear in battle;
I am the god who puts fire in the head;
Who spreads light in the gathering on the hills?
Who can tell the ages of the moon?
Who can tell the place where the sun rests?

(This translation is from *Gods and Fighting Men* by Lady Gregory.)

"*The god who puts fire in the head*" is thought to be poetic inspiration. The last three lines are a riddle, the answer of which could be "Who but I?" - as the person who has become a living, thinking part of their environment.

82

MASKS

Masks are alive! We often see masks as things to hide behind, but they can also be creations that allow other ideas to take shape, to move and to present a different view of the world to us humans. With **Crazy Hats and Hairdoes**, we can disguise ourselves and with **Story Shields** we can express our links with the world we live in, but when we work with masks we become that world and through masks we can let that world speak.

Masks have had many roles in many cultures over the centuries and any library should offer books that will tell the historical and cultural stories of the mask. Masks have been used for good and ill, to heal and to intimidate and to represent everything from ancestor spirits and elemental forces to animals and deities. Essentially, their role is always to transform the wearer. In traditional courts in Malawi, for example, a human could not be tried for any action performed while wearing one of the Gule wam Kulu masks of the Nyau societies because when masked, the dancer is no longer "human" and "accountable". When we who are not masked meet a mask-wearer we can have a chance to communicate with something usually voiceless.

In our work, masks offer us one of the strongest of identifications with the natural world.

Nyau dancer, Malawi

83

When we make masks, a whole character unfolds beneath our hands full of its own strange passions and unexpected humour. When we go on to work with masks in performance, it is not our familiar friends before us, but these Other People and it is their world we will meet.

Working sensitively with masks can allow us to step out of our humanity and in a controlled and dramatic way see the world from other perspectives. We can learn to leave our human-centred preoccupation behind and appreciate more personally the needs of the rest of the world.

This chapter offers some simple basic mask techniques and then a range of developments either from that starting point or drawing upon activities described in other sections of this book.

Leaders' Notes

Materials: as well as the standard "Basic Kit", the following are all useful additions: lots of elastic: 3mm or 6mm approx. widths (allow about 25cm for each child), several staplers and/or lots of paper fasteners (up to 10 - or more -for each mask) eyelet pliers or a single-hole punch
Time: allow at least 1.5 hours for a simple session, more time allows for more elaborate masks and more developed performance
Organisation: an activity for individuals working together - each person should have the chance to make their own mask but if they do not want to, to help and then support someone else in performance is a possibility.

Hints: paper fasteners - invaluable for holding things together - quicker than glue and easier than stapling through card - make sure the "legs" open out away from the face.
paint/pens - use with discretion if you want to get people working with natural materials. Try withholding until the final moments when they can be used to add finishing touches.
encourage variety - use natural materials for texture and even sound as well as colour - what suits the mask?

Indoors - or where natural resources are limited have a stock of useful things available - sheep's wool, sea-shells, dried pulses, cloth scraps, odd things from scrap stores or home - corks, bottle-tops, carrier bags (to shred) cotton reels...

GETTING STARTED
Draw people in gently - don't just give them a piece of card and tell them to make a mask! Give your group time to explore, to get the know the place, the animals, the feel of whatever you hope to make masks of. Use environmental awareness activities to really get to grips with the site. Experiment with simpler art forms - collect textures, create the shapes of the place, perform the animals (see **Body Sculpture**). Bird-watching, pond-dipping and mini-safaris could all give people the chance to study possible subjects more closely.

Then leave final choice of subject up to the individual - try a **Dreaming** activity, or simply start rummaging around and muttering. If someone does need guidance, go for variety and suggest subjects as yet untouched by the rest of the group. Don't impose your own value judgements about "good" and "bad" subjects - maggot and worm masks can prove to be amazing!

POSSIBLE THEMES
How about trying some of these?
Life in....hedgerows, fields, wood, soils - natural history/ecology based observation
The Secret Life of...playground, classroom, shopping precinct - nature and fantasy combined and unleashed
Weather - good for **Trickster Masks** in the changeable British climate
Life-cycles and natural processes - again good for Trickster ideas of change and transformation
Pollution - pairing pollutant and victim can give powerful drama opportunities
Other Problems - blue-green algae, big dogs in the playground
Single Topics - individual masks making up collective forms - all the pigeons who visit the playground, a flock of sheep.

SIMPLE MASKS

Here are 4 quick mask shapes to work with. For all of them, collect leaves, feathers and other natural materials or exciting scrap stuff to decorate them with rather than using paint and pens.

When you are working on your mask, remind yourself:

"where has this mask come from?"

- a pond, hedgerow, a tree, perhaps?

And wonder, as the mask takes shape:

"what sort of character is in this mask?"

- friendly, fierce, silly, foolish...?

1.Owl: fold down the centre and work on feathers with leaves or grass perhaps

2.Butterfly: fold down the centre - decorates well with leaves

3. Helm: make a cap of card strips and fasten on a faceplate. Cover the whole thing with leaves or junk - good for building up crests and streamers (try plastic cups and shredded carrier bags)

4. Bird: fold at the top corners and along the dotted lines, fasten the top corner flaps. Add a beak (or a square muzzle) and decorate

86

BEAKY MASKS

The technique used for **Giant Fish** can also be used to make large masks in the style of the peoples of the North-west Coast of North America

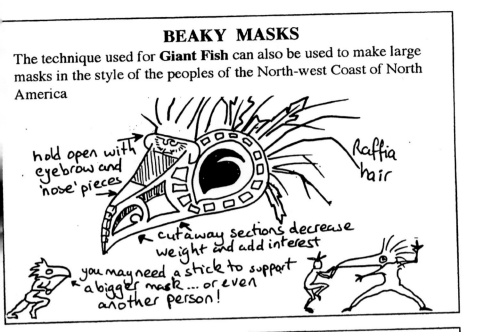

hold open with eyebrow and 'nose' pieces

Raffia hair

cutaway sections decrease weight and add interest

you may need a stick to support a bigger mask ... or even another person!

BLUE-GREEN ALGAE MASKS

These were a "special" used to animate the aquatic menace - working with **Simple Mask** shapes gave a wonderful opportunity for playing with textures

leaves + polystyrene packing chips strung on twine & plastic strips

grass 'stars'
rush and reed spikes
"sea grass" unravelled
glue-soaked string
carrier bags stuffed with leaves
SHAPES based on water plants, the effects of big algae & microscope pictures of different algae

seeds stuck on 'face'

TALL MASKS

Withy and tape can be used to build frames
to elongate necks and elevate heads.
Cover with tissue paper and glue (see
Lanterns) or with strips of paper or plastic

Apache USA ←masks — from → Dogon, Australia Africa → Papua New Guinea

FREE-FORM MASKS

The crushed and taped paper method of **Fat Fish on Sticks** can be used to build very versatile masks. Starting with a number of large, firm, paper "sausages" to make a cap or helmet, all sorts of things can develop.

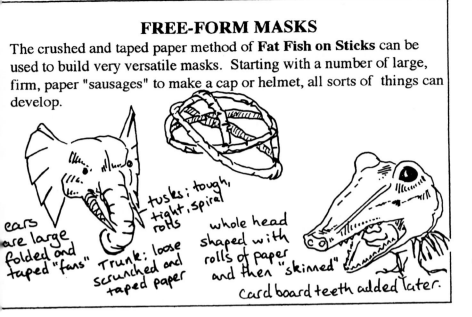

ears are large folded and taped "fans"

tusks; tough, tight, spiral rolls

Trunk: loose scrunched and taped paper

whole head shaped with rolls of paper and then "skinned"

cardboard teeth added later.

SCRAP MASKS

Go wild and experiment with a pile of interesting (and safe!) junk: anything you can see through, or out of, might become a mask - and everything else might become a stylish accessory for a Mask

masks: carefully chosen tops of large plastic containers (scavenge from "FLYING MASK")

HUB-CAP: found and washed; drawer handle and ribbons added

decorated remains of umbrella

TRICKSTER MASKS

Think of Nature as the arch-trickster. How much of what we see or encounter in the world around us is actually pretending to be something else? Camouflaged moths, a chamaeleon changing colour, caddis fly larvae wrapped in cases of twigs and stones, stick insects, a pale spot in the heart of a beautiful flower may unfold into a hunting crab-spider....

Trickster Masks work with that "what you see is not what you get" idea. Starting with some of the **Simple Masks**, build up layers of disguise that might be very straightforward - a crumpled sheet of pale tissue forms a chrysalis around a butterfly - or more complicated - one mask built over a second can open out to reveal a totally different face.

Trickster/Changing Masks can be fiddly to make but offer huge scope for exciting ideas and cooperation in performance as they may well need two people to "operate" them.

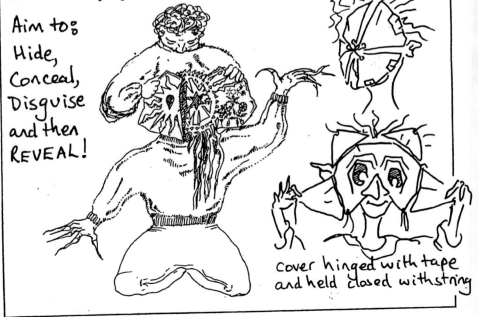

Aim to:
Hide,
Conceal,
Disguise
and then
REVEAL!

cover hinged with tape and held closed with string

Bringing masks to life

A mask once made that is not then used is no mask at all. To really come into their own, masks need to be "brought to life". We need to have them cavorting across the classroom, or hiding in the long grass of a field, or to be inside the mask that goes prowling through its own fantastic forest.

Getting masks going is a careful process: make the most of its dramatic quality and you'll call the strongest responses from your masked group. With well planned drama you can also remove any lingering worries about where role-play ends and reality begins.

Stage 1.Getting ready...

While people are making their masks, encourage talk about them: who/what is it ?...who/what are its friends?...where does it live?...what is its name?...and so on until the maker has a character forming in his or her head.

Stage 2....is on the next page

Stage 3....talking-out.

When a Mask is ended, or if someone simply wants "out", rather than just pulling their mask off, either brief people beforehand, or the talker-in can speak:

> ~ stop, turn away from any "audience" and relax.
> ~ breathe in, and as you breathe out, take the mask off
> ~ and become your normal everyday self again...
> ~ everything that was the Mask goes with it
> ~ and you are you, yourself again, and you are here, now, in
> this place, at this time, with lots of friends
> ~ place your mask down on the ground and clap sharply or
> stamp once to end the magic.

Stage 2. Talking in...

you don't just put a mask on, you become the mask you will wear.
This can be a little ceremony all of its own. A "talker-in" is needed:
someone with a calm, friendly voice, who can sound confident and
controlled. The talker-in speaks, and says:

~ *no speaking from now on*

~ *face away from everyone else. Stand easy. Hold your mask
in both hands and look at it.*

~ *trace its shape with your fingers, feel its hair, its eye holes,
its nose, its skin. get to know the shape of your mask*

~ *breathe gently*

~ *close your eyes and feel the mask as if it was your face: feel
your own face change shape so that it is exactly the same shape as the
mask*

~ *take a breath and as you breathe in, put the mask on*

~ *don't turn round yet!*

~ *now, Mask, look at your body, this new body you've just got*

~ *is it the shape you want? do you need to change it in any
way?*

~ *how about how it stands?*

~ *look at your arms...elbows...hands...what shape should they
be? Change how you move and hold them to suit yourself* (now work
right down to the feet - this is all usually quite silly, keep it gently
humourous.)

~ *and now, Mask, breathe in. And out. Feel your breath filling
all of this new body. Filling it with life!*

~ *breathe in, and as the air goes out again, does this mask have
a sound it wants to make* (they may squeak or grunt, whistle, snarl or
mutter - avoid full-formed human speech or we end up with people
wearing costumes rather than Masks, people from another world)

~ *and now, when you are ready, turn round....*

This sequence could be used for up to 7 or 8 people at a time and
leads easily into improvisation - a chance to play with the Masks and
let people, both performers and spectators enjoy the unfolding Mask
characters. (See **Improvisation Ideas** on the next page)

Improvisation Ideas

Here are a few suggestions to work with when your masks have been "talked in". You can try almost anything to leave your group at ease with and enjoying their masks. To begin with keep ideas simple and often rather ludicrous - the group can go on to explore stronger issues as they become familiar with their mask-characters and animating these.

Solo:

draw the Mask forward, toward a quietly sitting audience - encourage people to be welcoming and inviting. Encourage the mask to communicate - make small-talk (but to communicate, the mask does not necessarily need to speak)

> ~ *where has it come from?*
> ~ *has it travelled far?*
> ~ *is it shy/bold/friendly/grumpy?*

Enjoy this first meeting of different worlds. And then let slip some small gem about this particular Mask: perhaps it is actually an astronaut, a world-famous musician, opera-singer or popstar, the fastest milkman ever, an Olympic ice-skater. Could it please, go on you can do it, give us all a quick demonstration.
Be appreciative!

This is all great fun, but with a large group could take forever - so try a group improvisation with a few masks.

Going further

These improvisations are simple, usually great fun, generate a lot of laughter and are excellent for developing familiarity with mask ideas. To take things further, try using some of the activities described under **Move It!** and draw upon the characters that people have devised and the original theme behind the mask-work. **The Council of All Beings** lends itself very well to mask work and mask performance in its climax.

THE COUNCIL OF ALL BEINGS
A scenario that builds into powerful performance and needs careful
handling.
.......the living beings of the world gather - the animals, the plants, (and
maybe the earth, seas and skies as well); and in their council circle they
talk about their feelings. What is happening to them? What are humans
doing to the Earth? What are their feelings towards humans at this time?
What would they like humans to do to mend the hurts that have been
caused?

   And human representatives come to the Council to speak of their
understanding (or lack of it) and to listen and to make their own personal
pledges to start to heal the wounds and bridge the gulf between humans
and the Council of All Beings.
This is a potentially explosive situation and handles some very deep
emotions: you need to work without judgement and condemnation but
always to be building towards positive outcomes rather than, despairing
outpourings.
Work through the book *Thinking Like a Mountain* by John Seed for a
complete background to the idea of this workshop.

MOVE IT!

It can be very comforting to settle down in the middle of a field with a pile of glue, scissors and stray bits of elastic to create something wonderful with your group. The thought of actually getting up with a group, however, and trying to use bodies and movement to express discoveries can leave the strongest leaders quivering in their hiking boots. Movement, rather than word-based performances, are often relegated to "I want to be a Tree" parodies (and in shaping that, the line should be "I am a Tree"!) but to use a lot of the other activities in this book you, as a leader, can benefit greatly from being comfortable leading a movement session.

It is not very hard - it requires less materials than almost anything else: when you are comfortable with the ideas, you can slip into a quick movement session almost any old time. It just needs you to have the gall to stand up and suggest things to people. Using movement to express our feelings is a very natural thing to do - we do it all the time. Here, however, we are simply organising that body language a bit more and expanding the vocabulary a bit. It is natural and powerful and combining it with rhythm activities and perhaps with improvised instrument

A thought for dancing with:
"Ah, but they could dance! Nobody danced like the tigers, nobody could even think of such dances as they did. Moon dances, shadow dances, silence dances, dances for the starlight and the glimmers on the river. Even the child tigers among them danced the most complex patterns and difficult rhythms in the bending grasses and the shadows of the jungle under the hissing and humming of the moon, under the racing clouds, under the teeming rain."
from *The Dancing Tigers*, by Russell Hoban and David Gentleman

workshops, connects us to a living tradition that reaches back in an unbroken line to our very earliest ancestors. If it makes you happier, do not even think of it as dance: think of it as a walk with a bit more bounce.

Dance is a joy and a wonder and a release - quite possibly giving a greater sense of achievement in more people than many of the activities given in this and other books. In our society so many people grow up knowing (because they've been told) that they cannot dance (or sing, or draw, or play a musical instrument) - or that dancing fits into certain prescribed formats - it has to be folk, country, club, jazz, disco or what-ever. We rarely have the opportunity to reach out to the world around us and use our bodies as the expression of what we find there. The strength of response we find in our hearts during such a workshop can be startling - often more so in adults than in less inhibited children.

> ### Key points in movement
> ~ relax your self and your group
> ~ slow down! and do everything twice
> ~ listen to your breathing
> ~ let your breath suit whatever shape you are
> ~ as a leader, enjoy it
> ~ help your group enjoy it
> ~ don't call it "dance"

In this chapter, we shall just touch upon the edges of potential movement work- here are activities to get people moving and to put together quick performance pieces. Activities here may also help with work with masks, puppets, hats and some of the other things that you might create that then need performance to reach their full potential. Longer and more sustained activities are explored in the book "Sacred Animals".

If you are wary of all this, look on it as a challenge. Try out the activities yourself, or with a friend or two (or your whole staff?) and enjoy them. Have a good laugh and listen for the time when laughter changes from that of embarrassment to that of delight and achievement.

Leaders' Notes

Details of "Time" and "Organisation" are given with each activity. Materials on the whole are minimal. The use of music is very much up to you and your situation. Lugging a hefty ghetto-blaster out into the middle of a field and then having the batteries die on you is not much fun but often some good background music can fire up a movement session much more than relying on the sound of feet on earth or floorboard (strong and exciting in themselves, but for a cautious group music can help people let go and get on with it).

Music has to be chosen with care - some of the pieces I use are given with the Bibliography. What you go for is up to you but listen for a strong rhythm that can still allow for a variety of responses in movement, giving space for individual interpretation within your group. In general, I avoid popular music, going for more obscure pieces where people will respond more to the music itself than their existing feelings about it.

WALKING

Time: 5 - 10 minutes
Organisation: whole company

Try walking around - but walk with different parts of your feet touching the ground first

     normal - heel first
     toes/ball of foot
     outside edges of feet
     inside edge of one and
outside of other foot
     backwards - heel first
     backwards - ball of foot
first

Use this to exaggerate your whole body's movement. Do some walks become naturally stealthy, sinister, confident, timorous, ridiculous?

LEADING YOUR BODY

Time: 10+ minutes

Organisation: whole company

Go on from **Walking** to lead yourself with other parts of your body.
Start by walking normally - which bit of your body "leads" - which bit
takes you forward? - your feet, chin, chest?

Try walking now as if there is a string attached to the particular piece of
your anatomy and that it is gently pulling you along after it - or perhaps
find that all your senses are concentrated not in your head but in that bit
of body and like a strange nose it is wiffling onwards with the rest of you
following on behind.
Try fingertips, elbows, knees, toes, hips, chest, chin, ears, bottom,
wrists....

See what happens to the rest of your body as you move - does your
breathing change, what do you think your body language says about you
now, what does this movement feel like (graceful, adventurous, fearful,
bold, angry?). Does any particular movement make you think of an
animal and its way of movement, or perhaps a plant's slow and sinuous
growth or even a snowflake drifting on the wind.

CONNECTIONS

Time: 10 - 15 minutes

Organisation: whole company

As Leading goes on, call for some "connections". Perhaps whenever a
drum beats, or the music pauses people must connect up with someone
near them - making contact through the leading bit of their body at the
time and there they must introduce themselves or turn and change direction.
Take Connections further by following someone: link up to your partner,
pause while you both match breathing so you are breathing together and
then set off - slowly and gently. Try to think of yourselves, not as
"leader" and "follower" but as two parts of the same animal. Using one
hand as the link allows the follower to have an arm free to move. Try

98

linking at the shoulder, or better still, with the palm of the hand low down on the leader's back: flat against the top of their pelvis is a good spot (more or less where the belt of a pair of trousers lies). Or, best of all, rest one hand on the back of your partner's and move on, being lead on a slow, graceful dancing walk, with your eye's closed while your partner sees for both of you.

TURNING
Time: 5 minutes
Organisation: whole company
Relax and walk normally (probably better off without music for this one), and on every fourth step link arms with someone and turn with them to change direction. Keep walking.
Let this rhythm get established and then pick up speed and start calling tighter changes: turn on every third and then second step. Finally, people should be in a close group turning on every step - a sort of disorganised "grand chain" out of folk dance.

CONNECTED GROANING
Time: 10 minutes
Organisation: whole company, working in pairs, groups and all together
Working with body and voice, this is a nice activity to relax everyone into giggles to end one phase of a workshop while also being a good physical contact activity. If tied in with **Vowels**, the "groans" become much more musical and can help to thoroughly open up the airways for other vocal work.

Lean against a partner and have a good sigh. Match your breathing and let your sighs deepen and gain voice to become full fledged groans. Feel the vibrations of your groan in the bones and muscles of your chest, use it to let your limbs feel warm and relaxed, and to throw away any worries that you do not want to clutter up your thoughts during this activity.

Have another groan.

Without ever standing away from each other, try moving around your partner and groan against each other from different places: back to back, front to back, side by side, facing shoulder to shoulder, draped over each other.

Go on to groan against each other in groups!

SHAPES
Introducing ideas of "neutral" and "active" space: the difference in a person's stance that changes them from "saying nothing" to making a clear, eyecatching statement.
Time: 10 - 15 minutes
Organisation: whole company (or smaller groups)

Start with everyone standing in "neutral" - feet shoulder-width apart, hands and arms relaxed by your sides, knees slightly bent, head facing forward. Overall, this should be a relaxed position where something might be about to happen but certainly is not doing so yet!

At a given mark - a voice, a count, drumbeat or a piece of music perhaps, look up and around and curve your body into the shape of something you can see. The flow of a treetrunk, an individual branch, a bird, the splay of a leaf. Keep it gentle and slow. Practise the movement a couple of times.

Take it in turns to show each shape to the whole company who then shape it themselves and show it back to you. Always return to Neutral between shapes.

WINKING
Time: 10 minutes (but depends on the size of your group)
Following on from **Shapes**, we can now start building little performance pieces. Appoint a "conductor" who will wink at individuals in the

company at random. On being "winked" you flow from Neutral into your shape and hold it. When the conductor has triggered the whole company, he can then start "winking down" - cuing people to return back to Neutral again.

Variations: 1. Start Winking with the company in a circle - it follows neatly on from **Shapes** like this. But then scatter the group into a random pattern and try winking people into shape like this. You need to make sure everyone can see the conductor. 2. Once each person has made their shape, instead of waiting to be winked down, they could move back into Neutral when they want to. This gives a more dynamic effect with the group moving and changing all the time. 3. Use winking to trigger performance for Body Sculpture pieces as well so that instead of a large number of individual people changing there are a few larger movements growing and then dying away into stillness again.

When you are Winking with a group, you realise that "Neutral" is actually a statement in itself: a group of people in a neutral position at once create an atmosphere and their stillness will calm and concentrate any audience's attention.

UNFOLD, UNCURL
Another "shaping" activity, with a bit more to it than **Shapes**.
Time: 20+ minutes
Organisation: changes with the stages given below
Stage 1: start from somewhere low to the ground and curled up. Be as small as possible: crouching perhaps or actually rolled as a round pebble on the earth. Here think about the theme (see below) - try to let pictures of it run through your head.
Unfold from this small, still shape into a reflection of the theme - you might rise up and stand, or spread out along the ground. Try building a spiral into your movements - a curl or twist of your body as you change. It adds variety and energy to your change and much movement and growth in nature contains that feeling of unfold, uncurl, spiral.
Practise your movement a couple of times until you can go from your

neutral shape to your active one easily.

Stage 2: teach your movement to someone
else. Don't talk about this, just let them start
beside or behind you and follow your movement as you make it. Then you can learn
theirs.

Stage 3: if the two of you now team up with
another pair, go on to learn each other's
movements. Try putting all of these together
into a sequence and create your own interpretation of the theme.

This is a good activity for uniting individual
ideas and gives a final performance that is
usually more active than the more solid
constructions of **Body Sculpture.**

Some themes to try: seasons of the year (eg a
group of winter people, or a group of four different seasons), birth
(groups as seeds, eggs, wombs, spawn), the place around us (a bit like
Shapes), other themes given in **Body Sculpture** below.

BODY SCULPTURE
A very versatile activity that can lend itself to all manner of uses. Here,
a group of people use themselves to give a shape to an idea. Encourage
people to think of catching a moment or a single shape that sums up the
experience as completely as possible. You might discuss ideas about
emotion or atmosphere as "shapes" to free people from thinking too
literally about what they are going to do.
Time: 20 - 25 minutes
Organisation: work in groups of 4 - 6

The group stick themselves together, see themselves as a lump of clay,

102

shaped by the advice of the "director". Take it in turns for each person to direct a sculpture. The Director can move arms, legs, change body positions and shapes to form a tableaux before she then fits herself into the scene. Extra limitations can be added to the procedure: no/a little movement permitted in final sculpture, sounds from a soundscape could be incorporated or perhaps the director has to be separate from and be herself observing the final piece.

When everyone in a group has shaped their sculpture sort them into a sequence that allows the group to move easily from one shape to the next and present them as a performance.

Possible themes to try:
Personal Trees
symmetry (try geometric shapes before trying animal & plant ones)
Boggarts (they get everywhere. See **The Boggarts' Gifts**)
an animal we have seen (and can anyone else identify it?)
weather
landscapes
a special moment in my life

A COLLECTION OF FISH

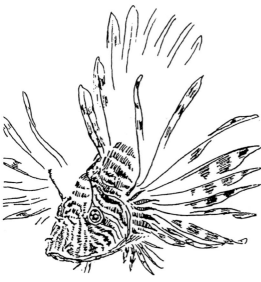

This chapter is about fish, for no particular reason at all. Here is an assortment of various modelling techniques which all lend themselves to spectacle of one sort or another - the common theme of fish simply links the ideas. They are all versatile enough to be used for lots of other subjects! In preparation, you could look at fish - in pond, aquarium or book. Examine them for colour and pattern, shape, movement, the texture and fine detail of their scales, the variety of their fin shapes. Enjoy them. Write **Haiku** to capture the essential "feel" of fish.

Leaders' Notes

GIANT FISH - for spectacular carnival or masquerade processions - and great for hanging from high ceilings afterwards!

Materials: basic kit, 2 large pieces of card and some smaller scrap for each fish, paint, plastic or cloth strips (bin-bags are useful)
Time: allow 2 - 2 .5 hours per fish - a bit longer if there are a lot of people trying to make their own
Organisation: these are very much one person products to wear although a couple of people working together could help each other make their own fish
Variation: avoid paint and encourage your group to use natural materials to colour and pattern the finished fish

add cardboard supports on the back to hold the whole fish open, don't bother with a cap, string the whole thing on rope like a pair of braces and wear the fish around your middle

and if not fish, then anything else! Lions, elephants, whatever - the design works best with rounder shapes, although longer, thinner ones can always taper down the wearer's back.

FLYING FISH - a lively use for old plastic bottles. A sort of rubbish dump version of **Fishy Windsocks**, Flying Fish animate well and lend themselves to some very dramatic movement and performance work.
Materials: basic kit, 1 clean plastic bottle per fish (5l or 2l containers for milk or orange juice are good sizes, see Variations below), cane or peastick or withy, waterproof markers (or tissue paper and glue), coloured plastic (old carrier bags are handy here)
Time: 30 mins - 1 hour
Organisation: an activity for individuals and the initial trimming, especially of tough bottles and cutting slots for the supporting stick can be time-consuming
Variation: almost any tubular form can be used - the larger containers give good chunky fish, but shoals of small fish made from toilet rolls and mounted on branching twigs can also be effective; or large-bore gas-main, 2-person conger eels can add that "monstrous" quality to submarine drama

FISHY WINDSOCKS - based on traditional oriental Fish-kites, given time, these could be as elegant as the originals, but usually end up as vigorous, colourful and rather chaotic interpretations of any fish the group could think of. While shapes can be varied, these derive originally from carp and goldfish and an initial encounter with these can be helpful - a visit to local water-garden perhaps to look at Koi carp?
The guidelines here are either for a relaxed, slower technique (**Fishy Windsocks 1**), or a more manic version for those occasions when time is pressing (**Fishy Windsocks 2**)

Materials: basic kit, 1 fish per group (ie 2 body pieces + fins), paint or

paint-on dye or fabric paint, long bamboo cane, wet withy, string
Time: depending upon your previous preparation, anything from 1 - 1.5
hours (version 2), or 2 - 3 hours (version 1) - leaving timefor drying
Advance preparation: if possible, cut out and sew fish shapes first -
with older children, this could also be aprt of the activity itself
Notes: fish shape- make out of cloth - thin cotton can be found quite
cheaply and takes colour better than most synthetics and is still light
enough to fly well

colourings: ordinary ready mix paint mixed with PVA and water
dries stiff but even this will relax with use and is quite the cheapest
commercial option - you could also make your own stains out of natural
materials or try extracting plant dyes. Specific fabric colourings may
give a better finish but are usually much more costly and not necessarily
more fun.

FAT FISH ON STICKS - a versatile technique for building small to
medium sized models - larger sizes do become a bit unwieldy (use Giant
Fish or **Lantern** ideas)but you could readily make life-size horse-heads,
say, and for smaller pieces, this is great. The same technique can be used
with some **Masks** and **Crazy Hats and Hairdoes**
Materials: basic kit, lots of newspaper, extra masking tape, tissue paper,
a couple of peasticks and a stronger cane
Time: 30 mins upwards depending upon the sizes involved
Organisation: depends very much upon the size of the animal being
made, but essentially an individual activity
Notes: to add the final skin, paint a PVA and water mix (60:40,or more
glue than water) over the model and press strips or small pieces of tissue
paper onto this. With practice, larger pieces of tissue can be used but
always try to keep the tissue fairly smooth. Folds can be very effective
on some places, in some animals - at limb joints and where necks join
bodies for example. Final small details, like eyes, mouth and gill covers
can be built up as papier mache. While making sure that the tissue is
well-attached, keep glue to a minimum to avoid soggy fish that take ages
to dry. (For a longer lasting, but heavier, finish, the model could be
"skinned" with plaster-cloth and PVA/water although the above PVA
mix is fairly waterproof)

GIANT FISH, part 1

1. Draw a fish outline on one large piece of card - keep the shape deep and fairly simple. Cut it out and use it as a template to make a second shape - make sure the two pieces are "right-sides together" if the card has been printed on.
Set all these to one side

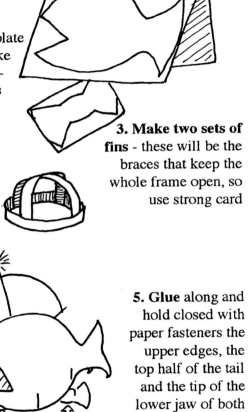

3. Make two sets of fins - these will be the braces that keep the whole frame open, so use strong card

2. Make a cap of thin card straps for your head - or use the inside of a broken hard-hat or cycle helmet

4. Before glueing it all together, a decorative dorsal fin may need to be added to the inside of one of the body halves

5. Glue along and hold closed with paper fasteners the upper edges, the top half of the tail and the tip of the lower jaw of both body pieces

6. Cut slots for the fins to slide into the body. For greatest strength, slit half the fin's distance in the body section and half in the fin itself so they slide into one another. Glue in place

GIANT FISH, part 2

7. Try on your fish. Jiggle it around so that it sits on your shoulders and you can see out of its mouth.

Fasten the cap with paper-fasteners (legs pointing out) so that wearing it will stabilise the whole structure without putting a lot of weight on your head

8. Support the fish on a bucket, stool or the back of a chair and paint it. Other materials lend extra effects - metal foil for scales, slender canes for fins and spines, old Christmas Tree baubles...

9. When it is nearly dry, glue or staple long strips of plastic to hang from the belly of the fish disguising your body and giving a feel of rippling underwater movement

FLYING FISH

1. Under direction, a grown-up should trim the bottle to a basic fishy shape and cut a small X top and bottom

2. Final shaping can then be done with scissors (depends on thickness of plastic) - look especially at the shape of the mouth and cut teeth if you want.....

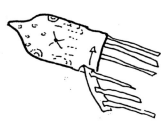

3. Decorate body with pens or glue and tissue paper - keep this delicate and look for a "stained glass" effect, especially with clear plastic. Watch out for the X cuts for the carrying pole

4. Cut some carrier bags up into long streamers 2 - 4 cm wide and tape these in a fringe to the back end of the body

5. Push cane through from bottom to top and fasten with tape. This might make a good support for dorsal and anal fins

6.And when your fish is finished, make it dance!

FISHY WINDSOCKS

FISHY WINDSOCKS 1

1. Attach small fins to each fish shape, then sew fish together along back and belly (you may need to get an adult to do this bit), inserting dorsal fin in back seam, and anal fin in belly. Keep right sides of fish together and do not sew up mouth or tail.

2. Decorate one side (see ideas below), and leave to dry.

3. Decorate other side - are they - should they be - symmetrical?.

4. Make a hoop of soaked withy to fit the mouth and bind ends together with string. Sew or glue into place by folding edge of mouth round hoop. Edges of cloth may need snipping to ease into shape. Glue or staple into place (glue reinforces the mouth opening).

5. Pierce 3 or 4 holes round mouth, attach string bridles and a flying string, tie to pole and display.

FISHY WINDSOCKS 2

1. Don't fasten fish shapes together.

2. Decorate opposite sides of each fish shape.

3. Staple side fins onto body then staple main body seams and large fins together (leave mouth and tail open).

4. Make a hoop of soaked withy to fit the mouth and bind ends together with string. Sew or glue into place by folding edge of mouth round hoop. Edges of cloth may need snipping to ease into shape. Glue or staple into place (glue reinforces the mouth opening).

5. Pierce 3 or 4 holes round mouth, attach string bridles and a flying string, tie to pole and display.

(**Alternatively,** you could sew fish shapes together in advance, decorate one side, slide a bin-bag down the fish's mouth to keep the sides separate, flip the whole thing over and launch paint at the second side. This usually results in the first side taking on a more unpredictable pattern than originally planned.)

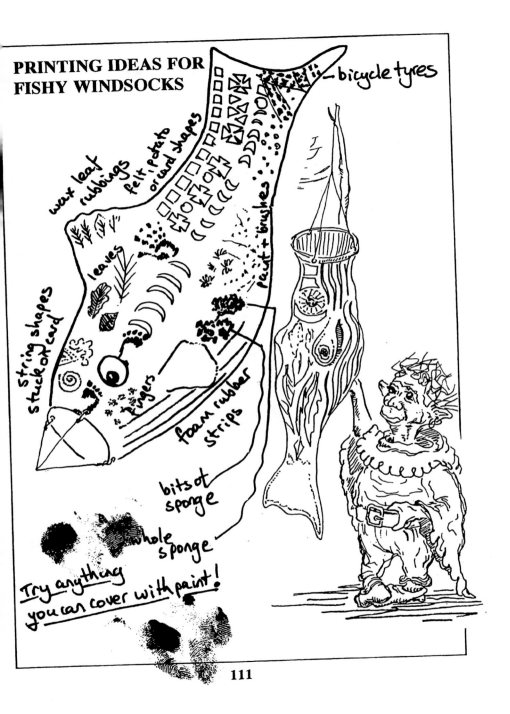

PRINTING IDEAS FOR FISHY WINDSOCKS

— bicycle tyres

wax leaf rubbings

felt, potato or card shapes

paint + brushes

string shapes stuck on card

leaves

fingers

foam rubber strips

bits of sponge

whole sponge

Try anything you can cover with paint!

FAT FISH ON STICKS, part 1

1. Scrunch newspaper into a tight, egg-shape and hold together with tape (don't overdo the tape)

2. Make this bigger by adding more layers of newspaper. Pack paper firmly but not too densely and again, tape in place. Think always of the shape you are heading for

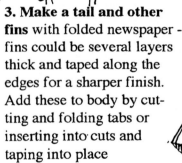

3. Make a tail and other fins with folded newspaper - fins could be several layers thick and taped along the edges for a sharper finish. Add these to body by cutting and folding tabs or inserting into cuts and taping into place

4. When you are happy with the shape, a final skin can be added by glueing on tissue paper with a mixture of PVA glue and water. You can use the tissue paper to build up fine details like eyes, lips and gills and even to get folds around hips and shoulders and so on on other animals

5. Allow to dry and then decorate - or decorate when wet by dabbing on wet paint, or flicking or blowing dry powder paint lightly onto the damp tissue...

FAT FISH ON STICKS, part 2

6. Now dig a small hole in the
fish's belly (this can feel very
unkind) and push in a cane to
carry it - you could make the
model on a stick right from the
start but this can be a bit awk-
ward. Or if you don't want to
be this fierce, hang your fish on
a string - from the end of a
stick, from the ceiling of your
room.....

Fish food: more adventurously shaped creatures with limbs
and tentacles can also be made. Legs work well if paper is
folded tightly into strips or rolls. Fine, insect-like limbs and
antennae can be made by rolling paper tightly round a peastick, taping the roll and then pulling the cane out of the
middle. Similar rolls could also be struts for insect wings,
with tissue paper or acetate film or tin foil "skins". For any
limbs or other appendages allow at least a quarter of the total
length for attachment to the body. In fact, the longer the
better - extra can always be trimmed off and a strong bond
gives a healthy limb, and the attaching of it can help to shape
shoulders and withers.

THE WORLD STANDS UP
- making puppets

The various activities in this book could be seen as a journey of experience into the world around us. We explore, grasp impressions and enjoy the adventure in **Getting Going**, and with **Dreaming** and the like, we go on to disappear into it with **Crazy Hats and Hairdoes**, proclaim our place in it - to anyone who notices with **Standards**, and to ourselves with **Mapsticks and Tokens**. All of this is a wandering spiral, winding deeper and deeper into the world and our hearts. And somewhere down there, we let the natural world look out of our eyes and talk to us through the mouths and actions of **Masks**. But with puppets, that world takes shape, independence and an animation of its own right before our eyes.

Puppets are also a joy and a delight of prancing clowns and outrageous dancers - like mimes, puppets present a mixture of the serious and the ridiculous. Puppetry is an ancient art taking many shapes around the world. Like masks, many cultures have developed their own distinctive styles of puppet theatre and the styles and variety of these offer rewarding study in their own right. We can investigate and adapt many of these styles to an environmental perspective, although in this chapter we shall deal with just a few simpler forms. Overall, you could look at:

>   **flat cut-outs** - flat card shapes moving back and forth across a "stage", maybe with some simple jointing, e.g. Victorian card-dramas

>   **shadow puppets** - flat shapes back-lit to throw their shadows onto a screen. These can be very simple or very intricate, with coloured inserts to give a "stained glass" effect and numerous joints for complex expression. Some of the most beautiful puppets ever perhaps come from the Indonesian Shadow Puppet theatres

>   **rod puppets** - these are supported by a main head stick (or held by hand at the head or torso) and arms, legs and tails moved by slender

sticks. Many of the Muppets of Sesame Street, the Muppet Show and various films are a combination of rod and glove puppets.

glove puppets - the hands that may be in full view with rod puppets, are here concealed inside the body of the puppet. An early act of animation for lots of people must be turning a sock into a talking snake or worm. For a more classical example, turn to Punch and Judy.

marionettes - for British children, alongside Punch, Judy, Sooty and Sweep glove puppets, these are probably the puppets that everyone knows. Suspended on and manipulated by strings, often subtly jointed and capable of a wide range of expression, they are also the most difficult of puppets to make and manipulate effectively.

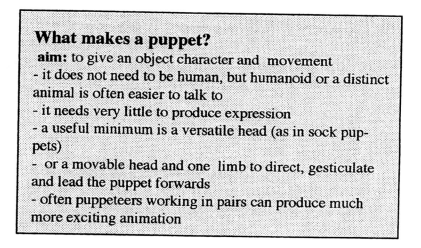

What makes a puppet?
aim: to give an object character and movement
- it does not need to be human, but humanoid or a distinct animal is often easier to talk to
- it needs very little to produce expression
- a useful minimum is a versatile head (as in sock puppets)
- or a movable head and one limb to direct, gesticulate and lead the puppet forwards
- often puppeteers working in pairs can produce much more exciting animation

In our work here, we shall be improvising rather than working with classical styles of puppetry; using ideas of animation to bring activity and character to whatever our groups find around us in our explorations.

Leaders' Notes

Setting the scene - the ideas used in **The Boggarts Gifts** can be a good starting point here to encourage a group to think about characters that might evolve out of the places and things they are encountering

Improvisations - as with **Masks**, when a puppet is made, it really needs to be used, to be allowed to stretch its twiggy limbs and jump and down a bit. The guidelines given in **masks** for thinking about characters and then initial improvisations can all be used here. Look also at **Practising Puppeteers** below.

1. GETTING ANIMATION GOING

TALKING SOCKS
Materials: at least one relatively clean sock from a foot (preferably one's own), scraps of sticky plastic or felt, scissors, some strong thread
Time: 10 - 15 minutes
Organisation: a whole class could work on this, with each person working on their own sock

TWITCHY WORMS
Materials: string, several peasticks
Time: 10 - 15 minutes
Organisation: pairs

STAINED WORMS
Materials: 2 pieces of scrap card (c. 15 x 12cm) for each person, staplers, paper fasteners, masking tape, one peastick for each person, not essential but useful can be a collection of various percussion instruments
Time: 30 - 40 minutes
Organisation: work in groups of 4 or 5 people

2. QUICK PUPPETS

3-STRING MARIONETTES
Materials: a squarish piece of cloth or fine netting (c 45cm square), string, or strong thread, scraps of card, glue, felt tip pens, scissors
Time: 30 minutes when built into explorations of the site, also add more time depending upon how much improvisation you want to do
Organisation: as good activity for individuals working in small groups, creating "families" of characters

SIMPLE ROD PUPPET

- a variation of the marionette, add one stick thick as a child's thumb and two slimmer ones, or a roll of cardboard wide enough for two fingers. The **Festive Goblins** described in **The Boggarts' Gifts** can easily become rod or string and rod puppets

3. GROWING BOLDER

IMPROVISED PUPPETS

Materials: almost anything! Have a basic kit on hand with extra peasticks and canes
Time: one hour, or more, or less
Organisation: small groups can allow individuals to make their own puppets or to work together on larger ones

GIANT PUPPETS

Materials: basic kit with extra gaffer tape, rope, withies and a range of bamboo canes
Time: usually several hours, or more, depending upon how much detail goes into the construction
Organisation: work in groups of 4 or 5 people to make the puppet - with very big puppets, you may need even more people to let the puppet move

TALKING SOCKS

pull a sock over your hand, tuck in a mouth, stick on a couple of eyes and have a conversation with the human whose arm you are attached to....or with the snake next to you

eyes made by tying sock round a ball of paper

TWITCHY WORMS

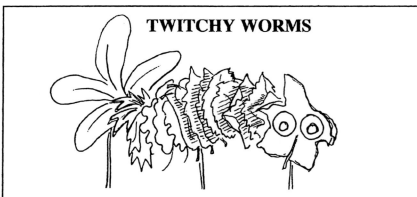

collect an exciting bundle of leaves, thread them close together onto a string with a stick at each end
you may need to add a stick or two in the middle - make sure you have a hand available for each stick!

STAINED WORMS

Start by finding some leaves that the light shines through giving bright colours and exciting patterns

tear a ragged hole out of the centre of the card

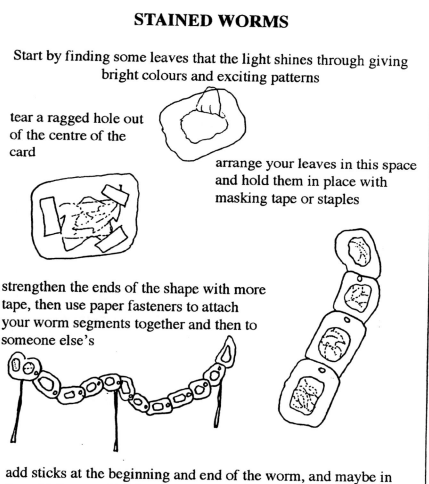

arrange your leaves in this space and hold them in place with masking tape or staples

strengthen the ends of the shape with more tape, then use paper fasteners to attach your worm segments together and then to someone else's

add sticks at the beginning and end of the worm, and maybe in the middle as wellmake your worm dance! try working in pairs to manipulate the worm, with the rest of the group providing music to dance to with stones, sticks voices and leaves, or other instruments

3-STRING MARIONETTES

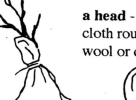

a head - wrap the centre of the cloth round a ball of newspaper, wool or dried leaves, tie with twine

hands - a pinch of cloth tied with twine with fingers of grass, roots or twigs add a face of card, decorated and glued on

the **body** can be decorated with leaves, feathers or grass laced into the material, stained with earth or clay, with necklaces of berries - don't let it get too heavy

make a couple of cuts and tie a loop onto the top of the head (or from the back of the neck) don't build too much foliage onto the top of the head or it is hard to manoeuvre

face drawn on paper and glued on

work your marionette with loops on thumb, first and middle fingers
make another puppet for the other hand

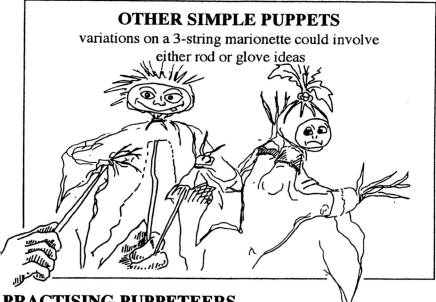

OTHER SIMPLE PUPPETS
variations on a 3-string marionette could involve
either rod or glove ideas

PRACTISING PUPPETEERS

To be a good puppeteer, you need to be good at moving your own body about, and working with other people without talking a lot, so try some of these activities (and some of the other ideas in **Move It!**) while your puppet is drying after painting or gluing.

~ balancing yourself along a log and try balancing other things on your hands

~ delicate movements: stay relaxed but still and see how much expression you can show by just moving your hands

~ with a partner, imagine you are glued together and try walking without falling over....try "glue" at your hands, or feet, or elbows, or your hand to her elbow....

~ imagine strings connecting you to a friend and take it in turns to be a marionette and a puppeteer

~ in a group play "follow my leader" while moving very close together. Keep changing leader

IMPROVISED PUPPETS

there are no rules here!

experiment with ways of moving heads and hands, bodies and feet

~ look at what things can become a "hand" - does it need to be hand-shaped?

~ does a "head" need to have anything other than some eyes and be able to move?

~ look at other animals for ideas

GIANT PUPPETS

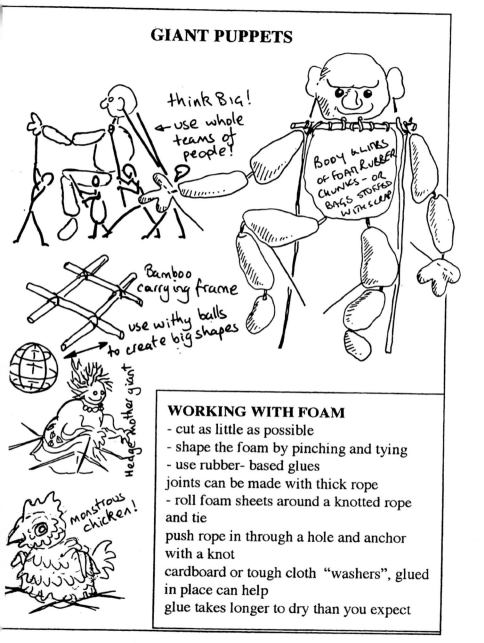

think Big!
← use whole teams of people!

BODY & LIMBS OF FOAM RUBBER CHUNKS - OR BAGS STUFFED WITH SCRAP

Bamboo carrying frame
use with balls to create big shapes

Hedge Mother giant

monstrous chicken!

WORKING WITH FOAM
- cut as little as possible
- shape the foam by pinching and tying
- use rubber- based glues
joints can be made with thick rope
- roll foam sheets around a knotted rope and tie
push rope in through a hole and anchor with a knot
cardboard or tough cloth "washers", glued in place can help
glue takes longer to dry than you expect

USING YOUR PUPPET

using your puppet depends very much on how it has been made but
there are some general points which can help draw performances out
of most puppets and puppeteers

~ look at **Masks** for ideas about characters in puppets

~ you do not need to hide - people will watch the puppet, not
the puppeteer - you can be invisible even when everyone can see you!

~ be as still as possible and very careful with your movements -
do not fidget or move unnecessary bits of yourself

~ relax! enjoy being a graceful, flowing shadow behind your
puppet

~ watch your puppet, not your audience. This helps them
concentrate on the puppet and is less frightening for you than looking
at all those people

~ think about looking out through your puppet's eyes: make
sure it is the puppet's head that looks, and the puppet's hands that
wave - not yours!

~ the puppet's hand and head movements are particulalrly
important- these tell the audience what it is doing and how it is feeling
more than anything else. keep these movements slow and clear and a
bit bigger on the puppet than they would be on you - exaggerate them,
but slowly!

MEDICINE SHIELDS, STORY SHIELDS

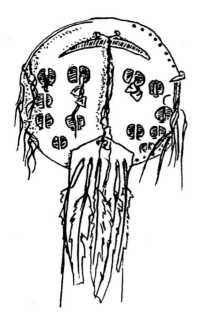

Alone on a hill-top, watching the night, listening to the darkness. A song, the whisper of a rattle - crying for a vision. A teenager stands on the threshold of adulthood, a chance offered to reach out for the dream that reflects the path that runs closest to one's heart and spirit. It takes courage to reach out for that Vision, and greater courage still to live out the patterns of the Vision.

Out of the North American Plains traditions of the Visionquest come medicine shields - physical representations of the Vision. A shield gives the Vision shape and takes the maker one step closer to bringing the Vision into everyday life. Shields are not necessarily war-shields to deflect weapons or blows, often the shield will be a painted disc of rawhide suspended within a decorated hoop frame light enough to be easily carried while the shield's Keeper is dancing.

Young people in our culture are rarely given such challenging rites of passage as the three nights and days of the Visionquest but making one's own Shield is still a powerful tool for helping people express for themselves the shape of their own relationship with the world they live in.

Like a **mapstick,** a Shield is a very private and personal artifact - it carries that same weight of personal interpretation. The imagery of colour, picture and decoration are entirely your own - no-one else can judge it right or wrong. Shield-making can come in at various levels of intensity - one example of a workshop is given under **Beavers, Crows and Mosquitoes** where Story shields were a group's tool to hold their own stories about individual plants and animals and landscape features. In other situations they might come in as reflective activities perhaps at the end of a few days of work, or after a residential course and might simply be set in motion by questions:

what have I learnt here?
what have I done?
what has happened to me?
how have I changed?
who am I now?

Or you could build Shields into your own transformation and growing-up "Rite of Passage". Such shields come closer to the original Medicine Shield where key elements of a person's Vision and personal "power" are decribed on their shield.

Leaders' Notes

STORY-SHIELD - the run-up to the making of a Shield is entirely up to you - **Beavers, Crows and Mosquitoes** was a whole day session and even this sent people away with final trimmings to add to their shield hoops.

Materials: basic kit, scissors, withies or a supply of flexible twigs - fresh willow and birch twigs work well, coloured wools, pens and pencils, twine - to string the disc with (button twine is a good size), shield discs.

Shield discs - traditionally made from rawhide, old drumskins are similar, or an effective alternative can be made from two discs (usually side-plate sized, but you could go bigger) of brown paper stuck together with PVA - tough and uneven like rawhide and strong enough to be "strung" without tearing too easily

Time: 2 hours at least - working on the hoop can be very time consuming

Organisation: an activity for individuals

Variations: as with **mapsticks,** you can always do away with wools and pencils and devise your own colouring materials from the local environment

DRESSING FEATHERS - a chance to make something special of feathers found and treasured on expeditions: this becomes a small activity in its own right, good for quiet times of relaxation and winding down. The resulting feathers are ideal for decorating Shields - or hairs, rucsacs, hats, each other....

Materials: at least one large-ish feather each (25cm+), several sharp knives (scalpels are good here, or small bladed craft knives), a bag of small feathers or scraps of sheep's wool, assorted bits of felt, needles, scissors, coloured cotton thread, lump of beeswax (or candle-ends), glue, thin twigs

Time: allow about 30 mins for a first feather in a relaxed session. The whole procedure can actually be a good bit quicker but it is good to take time and give people a chance to chat!

Organisation: an activity for individuals but with the whole group sharing materials. Make sure there are enough needles for everyone to sew.

ymbols for shields? Arapaho beadwork: 1: erson, 3: caterpillar, 4: swallow, 5: spider, 6: iver; Blackfoot beadwork: 2: person; SE USA: 7, : birds, 9: cloud, rain & lightning, 10: rainbow cloud; 11: general: horse, buffalo, boar, bear; odern Manchester: 12: mice, 13: bird

MAKING A STORY SHIELD, part 1

When you know the story that will go onto your shield, decide on its most important moments or characters. Draw these onto your shield - they do not need to be "realistic" - as long as you know what your drawings mean, they could be as abstract as you choose

Bend the withy gently into a hoop big enough to leave about a 5cm gap around the the disc. Overlap and fasten the ends of the hoop together with wool, twine or tape. A string across the middle will help the hoop hold its shape while it dries

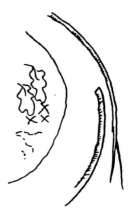

Pull each stitch tight and push together

Wrap wool round the hoop - using colours to help your story along. Either just wrap wool tightly round the withy, or you could do a "buttonhole" stitch for a stronger finish

MAKING A STORY SHIELD, part 2

Use the points of your scissors, or of compasses perhaps, to make holes around the edge of your disc. Now use the twine to lace the disc into your hoop. Get someone to help you hold everything together. Thread the twine through the holes and over the hoop but do not pull very tight yet

Try to position the disc in about the middle of the hoop and gently work round the disc pulling the twine tight. Then tie off the twine. To be most secure, a disc needs to be laced in all the way round its edge but if you are in a hurry, 6 or so separate loops could be used to hold the disc in the hoop.
Add final decorations to the hoops: tufts of leaves, grass, wool, feathers - whatever suits your story. Tie on a loop to hang your shield from.

DRESSING FEATHERS

1. Stand your feather in hot water for 10 or 15 minutes to soften the end

2. Carefully cut a scoop out of the bottom end of the feather. Don't cut right through the shaft and don't cut off the tip

3. Put a drop of glue in the hollow of the main shaft and fold the tip so that it tucks inside the main shaft. Tie some thread round the joint to hold the tip in place

4. With glue and thread, decorate the end of the vane with a feather fluff or a tuft of wool

5. Cut out a square of felt big enough to wrap round the feather shaft with a little overlap. Glue one side to the shaft, wrap the felt round and then sew down the overlap and bind near top and bottom with brightly coloured thread

Hints: make sure you leave the loop free to thread a thong through before sewing, draw your thread across a lump of wax: the waxy coating should help stop it knotting up

BEAVERS, CROWS AND MOSQUITOES - a shield workshop

Aim: to use traditional stories of the shaping of landscapes and the nature of things to work on a "local folklore" of "why" and "how" stories

Activities used: wordstuff activities, environmental awareness walks, shields to capture and shape personal stories

Stories used: usually two of the following:
> *How Beaver Stole Fire From The Pines* - this plots the course of a river and the distribution of trees across a landscape
> *Why Crows Are Black*
> *The First Mosquito* - the latter are both stories to describe the origin of particular features.

In keeping with the Shield motif, these are Native American stories: there are similar stories all over the world and the choice is very much up to the leader. You can often find local tales for the shapes of hills, the depths of lakes and so on.

The day: everything revolved around questions "why is this road so straight?", "why do frogs hop?", "what does a hedgehog dream of?". The idea is to keep people looking and wondering about things they possibly take completely for granted. Environmental awareness activities are invaluable here for the way they can immerse people in apparently familiar places and reveal whole new avenues of experience. Wordstuff is used to help children shape their own stories, picking their own chosen thread out of everything else and starting to shape their own story. Shields now begin to take shape, almost as a personal agreement between the child and the animal or place - "here I am telling your story in colour and patterns that only you and I understand and if we both agree, I can use our shield to tell our story to the rest of the world".

It might be argued that this sort of approach undermines a scientific understanding of nature. In practice this rarely seems to happen. Often natural history knowledge becomes built into the story itself - the imagination the story generates, firing a need for discovery. Stories touch people on quite a separate level from the organisation and precise knowledge that a scientific approach calls for and to neglect either in favour of the other deprives people of whole realms of experience.

Finally, you could also ask which approach for most children will guarantee a mosquito a second look and a deeper enquiry: knowing that this is a six-legged, four-winged insect biting me, or that this is part of the ashes of a giant who said he would go on eating people forever? Does either make a difference to the mosquito?

TALKING TO THE EARTH: WORKSHEETS

A set of 20 A4 size worksheets are available to accompany this book. Printed on heavy, white paper, these are designed as photocopy originals for use in the classroom or with your group in other situations.
Each worksheet includes Leaders' Notes for the activity on one side and illustrated instructions for that activity on the other.

Contact the publishers, Capall Bann for details.

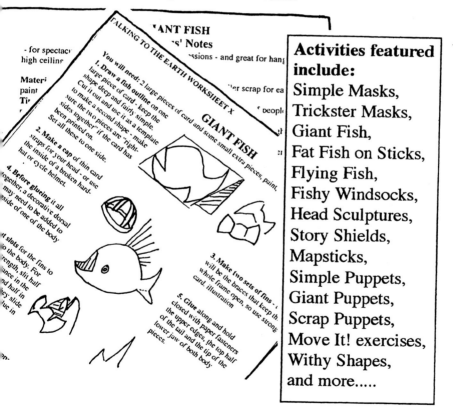

Activities featured include:
Simple Masks,
Trickster Masks,
Giant Fish,
Fat Fish on Sticks,
Flying Fish,
Fishy Windsocks,
Head Sculptures,
Story Shields,
Mapsticks,
Simple Puppets,
Giant Puppets,
Scrap Puppets,
Move It! exercises,
Withy Shapes,
and more.....

BIBLIOGRAPHY

Here is a collection of possibly useful books. These are some of those that I use: you also need to find your own books as we all respond to different books - explore bookshops and libraries on your own behalf!

INVALUABLES: books for inspiration in all directions
Coult, B and Kershaw, T: **Engineers of the Imagination**, Methuen 1983
Froud, B and Lee, A: **Faeries**, Pan 1978
Greig, S, Pike,G and Selby, D: **Earthrights, education as if the planet really mattered**, WWF & Kogan Page, 1987
Hoban R and Gentleman, D: **The Dancing Tigers**, Red Fox 1990
Hunt, W.B: **The Complete How-to Book of Indiancraft**, Collier MacMillan, 1973 (ignore the offensive comments about snapping turtles!)
Pirrie, J: **On Common Ground**, Hodder & Stoughton, 1987

GENERAL
Anderson and Hicks: **The Green Man,** Harper Collins 1990
Andrews, L: **Medicine Woman**, RKP 1981
Breedon, S and Wright, B: **Kakadu**, Simon and Schuster, 1989
Cahill & Halpern, **The Ceremonial Circle**, Mandala 1991
Chatwin, B: **Songlines,** Picador 1988
Goldsworthy, A: **Parkland**, Yorkshire Sculpture Park, 1988 (available from Common Ground)
Palmer, Nash and Hattingh: **Faith and Nature**, Century with WWF-UK
Seed, J *et al* **Thinking Like a Mountain** , Heretic Books, 1988
Walters, A, L: **The Spirit of Native America: beauty and msyticism in American Indian art**, Chronicle, 1989 (look for other books in the Chronicle series)

ENVIRONMENTAL AWARENESS
Cornell, J, B: **Sharing Nature with Children,** Exley Publications
        Listening to Nature, Exley 1987

Sharing the Joy of Nature, Dawn Publications 1989
van Matre, S (& Institute for Earth Education): **Acclimatisation**
Acclimatising
Sunship Earth
Earthwalks & Snow-walks folders
(contact IEE for a full resource sheet)

MAKING THINGS

Bain, C: **Celtic Art, methods of construction,** Constable, 1977
Caket, C: **Model a Monster,** Blandford Press, 1986
Flower, C and Fortney, A: **Puppets, methods and materials,** Davis
Publications, Inc,1983
Fraser, P: **Puppets and Puppetry,** Batsford, 1980
Joicey, H, B: **An Eye on the Environment,** Unwin Hyman with WWF,
1986
Learning Through Action: **We Are Of The Earth** (activities relating to
Australian Aborigines)
Mason, B, S: **How To Make Drums, Tom-toms & Rattles,**Dover1974
Petrash, C: **Earthwise: environmental crafts and activities with
young children,** Floris 1993
Welfare State International: **Lanterns,** from WSI (see addresses)
Wilbur, C: **The New England Indians,** Globe Pequot Press 1978

DANCE AND DRAMA

Brown, K, ed: **Sacred Earth Dramas,** Faber & Faber 1993
Fairclough, J: **History Through Roleplay,** English Heritage 1994
Hamblin, K: **Mime - a playbook of silent fantasy,** Lutterworth Press
1978
Heth, C: **Native American dance - ceremonies and societal traditions,**
National Museum of the American Indian 1993
Johnson, K: **Impro - improvisation and the theatre,** Methuen 1981
Lonsdale, S: **Animals and the Origins of Dance,** Thames & Hudson,
1981
MacLellan, G: **Sacred Animals,** Capall Bann 1995
Stolzenberg, M: **Exploring Mime,** Sterling Publishing Co, 1979
Woisien, G: **Sacred Dance,** Avon 1974

WORDS

Basho: **On Love and Barley: haiku of Basho**, Penguin Classics, 1985
Fisher, R. ed:**Witch Words**, Faber & Faber, 1987
Gregory, Lady: **Gods and Fighting Men**, Colin Smythe 1970
Jackson: **Celtic Miscellany**, Penguin Classics 1971
King, A and Clifford, S: **Trees Be Company**, The Bristol Press, 1989
 (available from Common Ground)
Llewellyn-williams, H: **The Tree Calender**, Poetry Wales Press, 1987
Maddern, E: **Story-telling at Historic Sites**, English Heritage, 1992
Nicholls, J: **What on Earth....? poems with a conservation theme**,
Faber & Faber, 1989
Skelton, R: **Spellcraft**, RKP

STORIES

Crossley-Holland, K: **The Dead Moon**, Andre Deutsch 1982
Erdoes, R and Ortiz, A: **American Indian Myths and Legends**,
Pantheon 1984
Garner, A: **Book of British Fairy Tales**, Collins 1984
Hughes, T: **Tales of the Early World**, Faber & Faber 1988
Juster, N: **The Phantom Tollbooth,** Lions 1974
Miller, M: **A Kist o'Whistles**, Andre Deutsch 1990
Riley, M: **Boggart Sandwich**, BBC Books 1989
Riordan: **The Sun Maiden and the Cresent Moon**, Siberian Folk Tales,
Canongate 1987
Sheldon, D and Blythe, G: **The Whales' Song**, Red Fox 1993
Sherlock, P: **West Indian Folk Tales**, OUP 1983
Yeats, W, B: **Fairy and Folk Tales of Ireland**, Colin Smythe 1973

LOCAL FOLK TRADITIONS

Briggs, K,M: **A Dictionary of Fairies**, Penguin 1977
Common Ground: **Apple Games and Customs**
Common Ground: **Local Distinctiveness**
Hole, C: **The Dictionary of British Folk Customs**, Paladin 1978

Jones, J and Deer, B: **Cattern Cakes and Lace - a calender of feasts,** Dorling Kindersley 1987
Sikes, W: **British Goblins,** E P Publishing 1973

MUSIC: perhaps even more subjective than books, to work from is music to dance to but these may give some starting points
Dancing Circles: **Beginners Dances 1**
                   Beginners Dances 2
                   Little Circles: dances for children - tapes of easy folk dances from around the world, with notes
Scott Fitzgerald: **Thunderdrums,** MO7 World Disc Music 1990
                All One Tribe, M25, World Disc Productions, 1993
Dougie MacLean: **The Search,** DUNC 011. Dunkeld 1990, - absolutely wonderful
Outback: **Didgeridoo & Guitar,** Maha 004, March Hare 1988
Mari Boine Persen: **Gula Gula,** RWMC 13, Realworld 1990 - team this with *The Search* for an excellent set of starting points
Gabrielle Roth and the Mirrors: **Totem,** The Moving Centre, 1985
                     Initiation, The Moving Centre 1988
Welfare State International: **Jungle Bullion**

USEFUL ADDRESSES: books and other supplies
P.H.Coate & Son, Mear Green Court, Stoke Street, Gregory, Taunton, TA3 6AY - supply withies by the bundle
Common Ground, Seven Dials Warehouse, 44 Earlham Street, London, WC2H 9LA: books, leaflets and inspiration on art, community and environment projects
The Crick-Crack Club, Interchange Studios, Dalby St, London, NW5 3NQ (story-tellers)
Dancing Circles, Wesley Cottage, New Road, East Huntspill, Highbridge, Somerset - DC tapes and many others - ask for a catalogue
Fred Aldous Ltd, PO Box 135, 37 Lever Street, Manchester 1, M60 1UX - suppliers of craft materials
Green Teacher (magazine), Old Station, Machynnlleth, Powys SY20 8BL

Hard Times: the magazine for play, Grumpy House, Vaughan Street, West Gorton, Manchester, M12 5DU

Institute for Earth Education, PO Box 14, Mortimer, Reading, RG7 3YA

NES Arnold Ltd, Ludlow Hill Road, West Bridgford, Nottingham, NG2 6HD - schools suppliers

Public House Bookshop, 21 Little Preston Street, Brighton, BN1 2HQ - source of wide range of books relating to Native American people. Write for a catalogue

Sacred Earth Drama Trust, c/o 3 Vernon St, Old Trafford, Manchester, M16 9JP - ideas and resources on using performance to explore the relationship between people and nature

Welfare State International, The Ellers, Ulverston, Cumbria, LA12 0AA

WWF-UK: Panda House, Weyside Park, Godalming, Surrey GU7 1XR - ask for education catalogue

INDEX OF ACTIVITIES

139

Sacred Animals by Gordon Maclellan

This is a book about animals, animals to wonder over in the Otherworld and in this physical world. Communicating, organising a sacred space, using words and chants, finding totems, the use and making of masks and costumes, body paints, music and dance are all part of communicating with animal spirits. These are all described here leading on to practical issues such as conservation and the integration of magic, ritual and practical hands-on action. Gordon communicates his love and wonder of animals, and of life with the enthusiasm and vitality for which he is widely known - a marvellousbook full of practicality and feeling.

ISBN 1 898307 69 5   £9.95   Profusely illustrated

The Wildwood King by Philip Kane

The Wildwood King is a unique workbook. Leading the reader through a series of traditional stories, ranging across cultures as diverse as Welsh, Russian, African and native American, and through a sequence of connected exercises, it facilitates a revitalised relationship with the Land. The Land in this context, is not merely our physical landscape, but also the natural environment and an aspect of consciousness. The folk tales of the world bear within them rich seams of wisdom. *The Wildwood King* sets out to follow one of these themes, to explore ancient understandings of the relationship between humanity and the Land.

ISBN 1898307 68 7   £9.95

Secret Places of the Goddess by Philip Heselton

This book is a practical and evocative encouragement to seek the Earth Spirit in those special places where it dwells, embracing a wide definition of Paganism to include all those inner yearnings towards a closer contact with the land. It will appeal to all who are drawn to visit such natural and archetypal locations in the landscape as tree groves, sacred springs, special rock outcrops, the seashore and the Wild Wood. All these are Secret Places of the Goddess. The author shows why certain locations have been considered numinous and magical and how we can each go about finding these special places in the landscape. He provides a vision of the variety of ways in which we might respond to the spirit present at such sites and thereby enter into a closer relationship with the Old Ones.

ISBN 1898307 40 7   £10.95   190 pages   Illustrated

Mirrors of Magic - Evoking the Spirit of the Dewponds by Philip Heselton

The image of the pond lies deep within our psyche. The abundant legend and folklore which surrounds ponds and pools, interpreted rightly, reveals the relationship which country people still had with the spirit of the landscape within living memory. This book shows that these "mirrors of magic" are locations where consciousness can be changed to experience the earth spirit and to perform acts of divination and magic. It also explores the powerful and recurring image of the Moon reflected in the still water of the pool and reveals how this has traditionally been used in magical ritual.

ISBN 1898307 84 9   £9.95   **R97**   Illustrated